Haley L. Scully

LAND
& SKY

FROM RELUCTANT BABY STEPS OF FAITH
(WITH ONE FOOT DRAGGING)
TO LEARNING HOW TO FLY

Land & Sky
Copyright © 2017 Haley L. Scully

Cover Design: Haley Scully, photo taken near Nelagoney Cemetery, Nelagoney, Oklahoma. 2015. For over 20 years, my great-grandparents, Monroe and Hannah Robertson, rented farmland near this tree. My Grandma Bonnie was born and raised near this land and under this sky.

ISBN: 1981854681
ISBN-13: 978-1981854684

To Dad and Mom
Every time I've said yes to God, you stood right beside me, teaching
me to trust Him, helping me believe, encouraging me to be brave,
and praying for me. You give me roots as my wings grow.
This story wouldn't be a story without you.

To Riann, Tiffany, and Sara
Who talked all of this out with me, a lot.

CONTENTS

"And you show that you are a letter from Christ delivered by us, written not with ink but with the Spirit of the living God, not on tablets of stone but on tablets of human hearts."
(2 Corinthians 3:3 ESV)

Introduction

Land

Most of my life, I've been looking for a place to Land. To me, Land signifies being grounded, steady, secure, to have dirt that I can stand on and run my fingers through and say *this is mine. I'm here. Planted. I have a place, a purpose, and a plan.*

I have longed for ground to stand on as evidence to myself and others that my life is valuable and well-lived. In full living-color, you can see it – tangible evidence that God is good, and that He has blessed me. In my mind, blessing comes in many forms – feet that walk beside me, supportive arms that wrap around me, little arms that rise up to me, and hands that guide me. Blessing equals people, places, and things. It comes with marriage, children, recognition, and success – not with mansions and gold, but with love letters, home, and family. Abundance.

Most of my life, I've been looking for a place to Land. Working, crying, and praying for a place to Land. Throughout my twenties, there was no clearance for the Land and blessing I desired. As I was getting closer and closer to 30, and my eyes were locked firmly on the Land I thought I wanted, the Sky began to grow dark with heavy storms filled with rain and thunder. Shadows of building clouds spread out over me and all the plans I tried to make. The wind swirled and tangled nearly everything in my life, until I began to lose the little grasp I thought I had. I begged for the sun to come out and shine on all of my hopes and expectations.

But the growing storm blocked out the sun. After staring at the ground for so long in an effort to gain Land, I was forced to lift up my eyes and turn my attention to the storm that seemed never-ending and unsure. Looking up was looking in the absolute opposite direction of everything I wanted to see. Looking up I could only see Sky, and Sky doesn't have anything firm to stand on. I thought the only option from up there was to fall.

Most of my life, I looked for a place to Land, until God gave me a taste for the Sky.

What's Your Story?

Have you prayed for your own version of "Land?" What have you wanted to receive from the Lord in order to feel secure and purposeful, or to prove His blessing in your life?

Have you been discouraged with circumstances in your life? Have you wondered why God seems to not respond or takes you in a direction you don't think you want to go?

Part 1:

Coming Out of the Wilderness

Clouds

The Land I wanted looked like my Oklahoma-born, Baptist-raised, good-girl-loves-her-mama kind of American Dream. Land to someone else may look totally different, but what I desired, what I believed I would receive and had probably earned, was a good life story. But, the life story I was living was not meeting my expectations or the order I had placed when I was a little girl dreaming of my *when-I-grow-up* days.

When the storm hit, and I finally had to deal with what my life had become, instead of waiting for my life to become what I wanted it to be, my turbulent journey from Land to Sky began. My focus was forced to shift from earth to heaven. Shift or die. Maybe not a literal death, although the storm felt that way. I could keep trying, figuring out, demanding, looking for, striving to work the Land in my own wisdom and strength, clinging to whatever seemed to be firmly rooted, or, as the furious wind began to lift me up, I could let go and rise.

The storm that was strong enough to make me release my grip came in the form of severe anxiety and panic attacks. My first attack happened out of the clear blue in an incredibly unfrightening place where being afraid would probably be the last thing on anyone's mind: Branson, Missouri – home of all things whittled, quilted, and accompanied by a fiddle and an "amen."

I had gone there with three friends whom I worked with every day and trusted like sisters. We were kind of enmeshed and dependent on one another because we had been going through a lot together. We spent our days in a workplace in which dysfunction and emotional instability were our wheelhouse. We were in and out of healthy, but we were in and out of healthy together.

Our vacation getaways were good. We all had different strengths and personalities that traveled well together. I booked hotels, printed out maps, and drove. Knowing that I had a penchant for being the one in charge, these friends let me be the plan maker and executor. Our closeness and trips were my favorite parts of our years together. Imagine twenty-something Golden Girls. That's a pretty good picture of us, and I'm pretty sure I'm Dorothy with a hint of Rose.

Our plans in Branson were going well until we walked down the first flight of stairs on our descent through caves at an Ozark Mountain family theme park. Ordinarily nothing is scary there except for the thought of the day coming to an end.

The only way I can describe the monumental moment that happened to me there was an overwhelming feeling that if I took another step into the abyss of that cave I would surely die. The panic literally gripped my mind and body.

The caves had been my idea. I felt no hesitation as we purchased our tickets into the depths of what would become the beginning of my despair. With each step downward, my knees got weak, my heart raced, and as I made myself look ahead to where we were going, I locked up and something deep inside broke loose. No warning and no explanation. I went to our unprepared khaki-panted guide and demanded to know the fastest way up and out.

My confused friends went with me up the stairs, and I could not stop crying as we sat on the nearest bench drenched in sunlight and fresh air. My body felt shaky and unstable for at least an hour or so after. I had no idea that was just the beginning of many long months to come.

It was like my body and mind had been looking for any opportunity to crash, just waiting for the moment when I didn't have complete sovereignty over the earth, its people, and circumstances. I had tried to be so controlled in every area of my life and everyone's life around me. It wasn't until I couldn't see ahead of me – I wasn't the tour guide; I didn't know where we were headed in that cavern – that the hold I had on life found a place to release. Once the dam broke, the flood roared.

●   ●   ●

"... as I made myself look ahead to where we were going, I locked up and something deep inside broke loose."

●   ●   ●

At first, the panic attacks only came anytime I felt out of control. If I was in (perceived) control, I could function, but if the reins were out of my hands, I would lose my mind. Back home in Tulsa with no caves around, the only place I didn't feel like I was in control was on an airplane. With my anxiety now looking for a new place to land, the only reasonable place where I couldn't control the circumstances was high in the Sky strapped into an economy seat and not in the captain's chair. Flying became my ultimate fear. I would hear an airplane overhead and panic, and tears would begin.

Eventually, the attacks became less and less discriminating. They just came on at will wherever I happened to be. The slope that had shifted downward was slippery, and I was sliding. I had nothing firm to grab hold of because I had been my own firm hold.

What's Your Story?

What do you rely on to have a firm hold? (job, economy, person, place, thing?)

Have you ever lost your firm hold?

Have you ever had to grasp for a new firm hold?

Fight or Flight?

One day my mind cracked a little deeper, and I reached my hand out in a new level of desperation as my panic reached a critical level of dysfunction. This time in Walmart. I not only looked scared, I also looked foolish – which was a double blow to my sanity. Who is scared in Walmart?

I was preparing for an upcoming flight to New York City for my boss' son's bar mitzvah and had a full-on panic attack while buying a mini movie player to help me stay distracted on the flight. I was ugly crying as I checked out because with each step of preparation, I felt like I was preparing to die.

I called my parents from the car on my way home. My mom cried with me as my dad decided that he was going to put his foot down and say that I could not go to New York. "You just call and tell them your mom and dad said 'no.'" (That line had gotten me out of a lot of tough spots growing up.) I reminded him that I was nearly 30 years old, and I could no longer use the my-dad-said-I-can't-go line to get out of things, especially not with my bosses.

Not only was this trip an expectation, but I also loved them and did not want to disappoint them or their kindness to me. Dad wanted to fix this for me, but he couldn't. However, the frantic nature of that phone call was a turning point for me. Dad reminded me that I did have a choice, and it was time to make it. The choice wasn't whether or not I was going to go to New York. The choice was whether or not I was going to let this panic control my life. So, I made that choice. I was not going to give in or give up. I decided to fight. In my own strength, which wasn't much, I made a plan.

Cue the fight music.

My plan was to go see Dr. Edwin Berger. I'm sharing his name with you because he was great. Dr. Berger was an old school doctor, who, in more than one appointment over the years, listened to me for a bit, and then with no words, walked out of the exam room to go grab a medical book. He would then come sit beside me, crinkling up the fresh slab of white butcher paper stretched out across the patient exam table, and get down to discussion with me.

Up on that table, side by side, Dr. Berger and I had talked about my gall bladder, a potentially suspicious mole, and my womb, which was "not getting any younger." In that room, with a framed print of the Hippocratic Oath hanging on the wall, I enlisted him to be part of my attack plan to get through and over this panic that was crippling me.

He talked with me and prescribed Xanax to help me get through the panic as needed. My heart was sick, my mind was sick, and that combination made my body sick. I was falling apart. Dr. Berger and I began to try to fix me, or at least keep me standing long enough for me to function.

I made it onto the plane and into New York City. The anxiety on the flights was brutal, but while my feet were on the ground, I was able to live … not abundantly, but I survived. I have great memories from that time with those friends, but it was all shadowed by the anxiety. I was able to function but constantly anxious and in emotional pain. Medicated functioning. Not healed, but being held still.

One of my friends was on a flight with me from New York to Chicago when I was medicated but still trying to hold on to sanity with white knuckles. When we hit a little turbulence, I lost it. I had sweaty death grips on my seat, and I began to cry uncontrollably. I did not win favorite passenger awards. People were annoyed and began to turn around and stare. My panic was not just affecting me; it upped the stress of everyone around me. My friend just gently patted me on the leg the way you would a child sobbing out of control. As she tried to soothe my shaking, she just kept saying, "If you were flying the plane, you would be okay."

These words hit the nail on the head. If I were flying the plane, I would be okay. If I was in control of everything, I would be okay. People in my life who needed me had put me in that position, and I had put myself in that position for a long time.

The decision maker.
The caretaker.
The straight shooter.
The one with a plan.
The fixer.

I've got me, and I've got you. I made decisions based on my own wisdom, moral compass, self-righteousness, and good sense.

Whatever the problem, I'm going to take care of it for you. I will carry your burdens because I am the strong one. When you are weak, I am strong. "Come unto me all you who are weary and burdened …" (Matthew 11:28a, NIV) Oh wait … that's a quote from Jesus. Not me. I thought my identity was in being the strong one. That was my value. That was my role.

The thing is, I was created and called to be a counselor from the beginning through God's gifting and equipping. But, I tried to operate that gifting and calling apart from my Creator. The enemy, whom the Bible tells us is trying to kill and destroy us with temptations and distractions, was able to distort that calling in an effort to destroy me with it. Unrefined and unsurrendered, my call to counsel, to lead, and to help others created a load impossible for me to carry on my own. I became bitter, angry, and depressed, until God in His great mercy allowed me to break on the way down into that cave. I can see His gracious hand in hindsight, but at that time, I was far from thankful for it. I became angry with a capital A.

At first, I tried to figure it out and fix myself. I did not run _to_ God. I ran _at_ Him. My reaction was to blame God for allowing this to happen, and I began to doubt His very existence. _If He was real, why would He let this happen to me?!_ I had been going through an emotional and physical crisis; now it was time for my crisis of faith. I was surrounded by people of little or no faith who were calm and on task, and I was apparently going insane. There was no fairness in what was happening. The God I grew up believing in would have protected me because He loves me. He would have blessed me for all the righteous things I had tried to do to live a good life.

I did not run _to_ God.
I ran _at_ Him.

To confirm my growing doubts, I looked at all that disappointing evidence in my life and thought, _If He exists, then why is everything so broken, and why am I not blessed?_ I believed I was a good person; worthy of blessing because of how I had (usually) tried so hard to do the right thing. _So maybe God isn't real. The Land I've been working doesn't show much evidence of what I should be receiving if He is who I thought He should be. I loved Him so much when I first believed. Why don't I feel that love now? If He is real, why am I losing control? Why am I forgotten? Where is He?_

What's Your Story?

What circumstances in your personal life have caused you to doubt that God is real?

Are there things in this world that make you doubt God's existence?

Have the actions of certain people drawn you away from relationship with God?

Cadillac to Couch

At my job in Tulsa, we used to laugh about my tendency to speak "frank" with people. The definition of frank is to be "open, honest, and direct in speech or writing, especially when dealing with unpalatable matters" (Oxford English dictionary). If a direct conversation needs to happen, I have never been one to shy away from it. I prefer communication over confusion.

Years after this point in my story, I was encouraged to begin writing to share with others what God was doing. So, I started a little blog. I didn't put a lot of thought into what I would name it, not realizing it would stick with me for going on seven years now. I reasoned, *Well, I want to write with transparency and be frank about the good and even the difficulties of this journey. Hopefully, I'm a bit more gracious now in my directness and frank speaking. I want to be both frank and gracious. Gracious and Frank, or Gracefully Frank.* The final name was the one I chose for my blog.

In February of 2013, I wrote a blog post reflecting back on this time from my "Fight or Flight" story in 2006. "Cadillac to Couch" shares the emotions and doubts I experienced at that time.

As my mind and world seemed to be coming apart, I often retreated to the safety of home with my parents. They were very much an anchor for me when I had yanked my own anchor up. I had been trying to fight the storm on my own, but this story details the moment I reluctantly agreed to see if maybe God would fight it with me.

Cadillac to Couch – February 07, 2013

The Cadillac. (Circa 1984ish)

I'm sitting in the front seat of a cream-colored, two-door, 1981 Cadillac Coupe de Ville with wire rims and cream-colored leather interior. It's night. It's just me and mom in the car. I can see a million stars looking out the windshield over the roof of our house sitting in the cul-de-sac on Oriole Street, and I just asked Jesus into my heart.

My 2nd grader heart felt fear and relief as I asked Jesus into it. In that moment it was real. I loved Jesus, and I knew He loved me, and now I was His. Saved. Check. Now, I push open that heavy car door with my right foot and go inside to take a bath and get ready for bed. Tomorrow is a school day. Whine a little bit, get my parents to bring me some water, tell me a story about leprechauns and rainbows (my favorite bedtime tale), and choose which stuffed animal would get to sleep in the big bed with me, curl up under my yellow Holly Hobby bedspread and go "night-night." A Believer. On the path of redemption with roads way ahead already preparing to diverge.

This was us, and that is the car I was sitting in when I asked Christ to be my Savior.

I don't remember the exact day or words, but I remember the exact spot where I asked Jesus to be my Savior. I still drive by our old house sometimes to reminisce about life there, and to see the mailbox my dad put in, and the tree in the front yard we planted about the same time I started kindergarten. It wasn't all that long ago.

We were church-goers. I don't remember Sunday School lessons about heaven and hell. I remember loaves and fishes. Giants and slingshots. Angels and a manger. Walking on water, and that Jesus loved me because I was a little child. But I don't remember being taught about hell. I do remember a few times tuning into a sermon about it as I sat in a big pew where my feet couldn't touch the ground. And I do remember lying in bed, listening to the alarm clock radio Mom and Dad let me have, where in my memory, "Glory of Love" is always playing, and my mind began to wander about heaven and hell. I remember thinking hell sounded terrible, but even heaven sounded a little bit scary. I didn't want to go so high up in the Sky and stay so long ... like, forever. I always pictured Ferris wheels in heaven, and I hated Ferris wheels.

But I liked Jesus, and every time they talked about Him, my heart would just about pound out of my chest. I wanted Him to save me. I did lie sometimes. I looked my parents in the eye without flinching and told them it was not me who put the loaf of bread in the microwave with the metal twisty still holding it closed, which sparked a fire burning the plastic bread sack all over the bread and microwave. It certainly was not me who just left it in there and ran. I'm pretty sure they knew the truth, but I didn't crack. I was a no good, dirty liar.

If lying was a sin, and sinners go to hell, and if Jesus saved sinners, I needed saving because I was a liar. I also sometimes said (said/say ... whatever) dirty words and went into my brother's room when he wasn't home and played with his stuff (specifically Luke, Leia, and Han action figures, and his Millennium Falcon), even though he forbade it. The depth of my depravity knew no end. But, a Ferris wheel would be better than a fire.

After asking Jesus into my heart and life, I remember being so excited to get to church on Sunday to tell my Sunday School teacher that I was saved! I finally did it! I couldn't wait to go down the aisle in big church and let everyone come by and shake my hand.

One of our Northeast Baptist Church deacons came over to our house and talked with me about what I had decided: that I was a sinner, and I believed who Jesus is, and I wanted/needed Him to save me. "For God so loved the world, that He gave His only Son,

that whoever believes in Him should not perish but have eternal life."
(John 3:16, ESV) So they scheduled my baptism for an upcoming
Sunday night, which Mom and Dad followed up with some ice cream
at Braums (how we celebrate in Oklahoma).

Then, I couldn't wait to get to school the next day and tell
everyone, "I'm SAVED!" However, neither I nor Jesus were the
scuttlebutt on the playground. A couple of my friends knew what I
was talking about, but no one really cared. They were lining up to get
a drink at the water fountain, not to shake my hand. *Uh…so who wants
to play 4-square? Anyone up for Red Rover or House?* This was one of the
first of many times I scooted Him back behind me.

I had asked for His life in me, and He gave it, but it would be
years before I would give my life to Him.

The Couch. (Circa 2006ish)

Mom and I were sitting on the couch still in our pajamas. Again, I
don't remember the exact day. We were a long way from that starry
night in the front seat of the Cadillac. I was in our living room in
Ponca City on a big, peach-colored couch in a room with mint green
walls and dark wood trim. My senior picture hung on the wall next
to my brother's, and it had been many years since the nails were
driven to hang them. I'm sure I was holding onto a pillow, as per
usual, and drinking weak coffee. I don't remember my exact words,
but as I spent several years sounding much like a broken record, it is
not hard to retrace my verbal steps.

I'm sure I reminded Mom of how much I used to love the Lord.

I probably listed my resume from youth group years: how I didn't get into that much trouble and tried to share Jesus with friends so they wouldn't go to hell. I recounted all the love I felt for Christ at Falls Creek Church Camp, where my relationship with Him grew each year. I always learned so much there, and surrendered to live my life for Him.

Actually, one year, I went forward to be the wife of a preacher. True story. I surrendered to be a wife. Cute. I knew God was calling me to live for Him and serve Him, but I was not going to go to Africa (which basically just symbolized all places beyond the borders of Oklahoma). I also knew I was not called to be a preacher. *So I must be called to be one's wife, to help him in his ministry.* Missionary or preacher's wife were my only known choices. Heart pounding out of my chest again, I went forward and surrendered to God and the husband I've still never met.

I'm sure as I sat there talking to Mom, I even confessed the years that I turned from the Lord and followed my own will. I knew I had sinned against Him in relationships and actions, but believed I was better than a lot of other sinners. I had repented of those things and lived as best as I could. I know that led me to a discourse on the reasonable doubt that God must not exist because I thought I had a relationship with Him based on all that I had done with Him in my youth. I had been trying to live a good life, but it still was not what I wanted it to be. *Where was He?*

I thought that having a relationship with God meant Him giving me the life I wanted, not about me giving back to Him the life He gives me. The Christians I was surrounded by (I was not in church but worked with some professed Christians) were some of the meanest people I had ever been around. The people of other religions, and of no faith, were the people I was growing in relationship with and saw their hearts to be good people.

I didn't see God in my life, and I didn't see good in people who professed God in their life. I was tired of the struggle. I didn't realize then that I was justifying and passing blame off on others for me not having a growing relationship with God. I let their hypocrisy be my scapegoat. I kind of don't think Jesus is going to say ... *Oh, WHAT? Are you serious!?!? They were hypocritical, so that is why you didn't follow Me? I totally get that. It's totally okay that you looked to their life to justify yours instead of looking to Mine.* I know that now, but it was a long road to finally see it.

"I let their hypocrisy be my scapegoat."

As my mom listened to me telling her that I didn't know if God was real and why, she cried. And, so did I. She's not usually one with a lack of words, but she didn't say much that day. I was a little unsettled she didn't try hard to fight me on it because I was ready with my defense. She knew I hadn't been in church for years, and the only thing she asked was if I would just commit to going to a women's Bible study like one she had been going to for a few years. She asked me to actually try to hear from God and not just the people I had been surrounded by. She was as discouraged for me as I was. She didn't lecture me; she just asked that I do a little bit more leg work before I called it quits. The road I was on was diverging again, and she pointed, didn't push, me in a direction that led to Life. She knew whose words I needed, and that her words wouldn't have worked that day. She went to Bible Study Fellowship, and there were a couple of women's groups that met in Tulsa. I told her I would go.

I sat by her in the Cadillac and prayed to accept Christ, and then I sat by her on the couch and renounced Him. – *Gracefully Frank*

What's Your Story?

Have you ever prayed to receive Christ as your Savior? What did you believe and expect from that prayer? Did your expectations come to pass?

Who in your life has encouraged your faith in God?

Is there someone in your past or present who is inviting you to a closer relationship with Jesus Christ? What are their suggestions? Have you tried applying their suggestions to your life? Why or why not?

Reverse Motion

So, I went. With a stiff neck and bitter gut, I went. I can vividly remember sitting in the pew with my shoulders bowed up and committed to not make eye contact or any sort of warm gesture that would make anyone think for a second that I was glad to be there. I said to the God of the Universe,

"If You are real, You are going to have to prove it."

(I actually said those words. My parents tried but failed to work the sass out of my mouth.) I'm not sure why He didn't just strike me dead right there in that pew. But He didn't even slap me. He just gently began to do exactly what I asked Him to do because that was already His will to do so. There I was, all grown up and hot with anger, and He responded to me as if He saw a little girl with hot tears desperately asking Him to help. His daughter was finally bringing her pain to Him. He showed me He is real and was there. It was as if He went to get His book and then climbed up on the exam table beside me to talk about it.

All of my years, I had been looking for evidence of Him in the Land I worked for through the actions of others or the struggles I faced. That was the exact opposite of the way I should have been looking for Him. As I tried to see Him-through-life, everything looked dark and distant. It was when I began to see life-through-Him that the stormy skies began to have some breaks in the clouds.

He had never left me, and the Holy Spirit was still with me, which was why He was gracious enough to never let me get settled in a Land so far away from what He had planned for me. He never allowed me to be content in the idols I had tried so diligently to be content in. He had become a distant voice as I traipsed across the Land I tried to claim. But His voice was still there. He never gave me what I demanded, knowing that I wanted those things instead of Him. He let me

*   *   *

"What hard and amazing love that allows the pain that heals."

*   *   *

strive and struggle and sweat until I broke like a fever. What hard and amazing love that allows the pain that heals. It was difficult to appreciate the valley of the shadows He had been walking me through.

The more my heart began to feel peace and reconciliation with the Lord, the more the idols and distractions in my life began to fall apart. For 10 years, I had poured myself into a job and people that I wanted to fulfill me – to give me purpose, significance, love, security, and Land. I thought the world and the people in it were holding out on me, being unfair and unjust. What I began to realize is that they couldn't fulfill those needs. It wasn't their fault or problem; it was mine. I belonged somewhere else. I had truly, in every sense of the words, forgotten my first love. With Him was where I was supposed to be.

Even though I walked on that Land in Tulsa, I was actually already committed to Someone. There were already plans for me way before I set out on my own journey. There was the One I had pledged my life to in the Cadillac, at the front of the aisle at Falls Creek church camp, and in my heart way before I could really even comprehend what that would mean. But, He wasn't even mad at me. He didn't hold it over my head to shame me. He just began to speak tenderly to remind me, to make me feel His presence and love again.

I remember describing it as being lifted up out of the fog and being able to see clearly again as I broke through low-hanging storm clouds to the blue Sky that I had dreaded. He began to lift me up out of a pit that I had dug myself – a pit in Land I tried to claim but wasn't mine.

He lifted me from that Land to the Sky, where things began to get clear. But instead of the firm footing I thought that would bring me, I would soon find out what relinquishing control would really look like. I thought, *Okay, I kind of went crazy for a minute to get me back on path, but I'm back, and now my Land will come. Me and God are all straight.* I reasoned that if distance from God had been my reason for the storm, then close proximity to Him should kill the storm and prevent new storms from forming. *Right?*

The first round of storms had been about my behaviors, my thoughts, and my distance from God. Getting back in His Word and around His people helped encourage me to change some habits, but it didn't fully change my heart. My heart motivations were still a lot the same as they had been: for me to get my best life in the way I understood a good life to be.

I would learn that there is a big difference in being out of control, and choosing to surrender it. After surrender, it's time to work on the heart, and there would be so many more clouds to break through before my heart would actually change.

What's Your Story?

Was there a time that you loved Jesus? Have you turned away from Him?

Have you already turned back? How did that happen? Is there someone who would benefit from hearing your story?

If you haven't turned back to Him yet, what might be your first step? Is there anyone you could reach out to and talk with?

Cleared for Take-Off

When I first turned my eyes back and up to the Lord, it truly was like a fairy tale. *You still love me? You are real and here and have plans for me? Great!! Let's do this! I will follow You, and serve in church, and now you'll bring my Land, a husband, and little church babies with Easter Sunday bonnets. Oh! And, I'll start living my job for You, and You will bless it!*

My work really did pick up at first. I had some potentially big deals at my job that looked like they were going to be financially advantageous. I thought those were signs of His approval of me and my turning back to Him. *Here you are, God, blessing me right away. You, big, faithful God, You.* I actually prayed, "Lord, help me know where You want me to spend this money. After I buy a new house and get settled, I will support missions or the retirement community where I help lead worship and a devotion on Sunday mornings. This money will be used how You want me to use it. In Jesus's name, Amen." My heart soared. *All is good. I'm back. Kill the fat calf!*

That's not exactly how things went though. Thankfully, He didn't reveal the fullness of His plans to me. In my understanding at that time, I'm 100% positive I would have said "no" to Him and stayed mucking around in the mud of my own plans. These plans I'm living out now would have been way too much. Too different. Too unrecognizable from the plans that I had wanted and made. That me, back in Tulsa, would not have appreciated the me that writes to you today.

The roots I thought had taken hold in Tulsa began to come up. That job I had given my life to for 10 years began to not be so welcoming.

Those big deals that looked certain, were not.
Those people I thought needed me, did not.
What I thought was my purpose in life, was not.

Bruised and confused, I told the Lord that I would go through whatever window or door He would open. Possibly for the first time, I truly began asking Him what His plans for me were, instead of just looking for Him in my plans. I told family and close friends that I was ready to leave and look for another job.

The sound of that first chain breaking was deafening. Resume with 10 years of experience in hand, I began the job search. I pulled up that first stake from the Land I had worked for to find my promised Land.

The interviews I went on led nowhere, and I began to see that taking a job that valued my experience would really just be lifting up the life I had in that current piece of Land and moving it to another. Same life, different Land. New building, new faces, same circumstances. *Is that the life I want after all of this? Is that what God has done this for? Was God breaking me loose from that* place *to just go to a new* place? Or, *was He breaking me loose from that* life *to go to a new* life?

With a broken and contrite spirit, I was truly seeking God with my whole heart. I was in fellowship and in His Word. In that environment, under those conditions, one day, I finally heard His call.

A friend stopped by my workplace struggling with heartbreak in a rocky relationship. She came to my office; I closed the door, and she talked while I listened. As I was listening to her, I heard Him: "Christian Counseling." Not audibly, not in a burning-bush-outside-my-office-window way, but inside of me – I CLEARLY heard those words. I honestly didn't even know there was such a thing.

Was God breaking me loose from that place, or was He breaking me loose for a new life?

After she left, I couldn't get those words out of my head. I wondered where you even find out about something like that. I knew about Christian schools in Oklahoma and knew about Southwestern Seminary in Fort Worth because I had friends and family who had gone to those schools. I looked up Southwestern online thinking maybe there would be a link to information. As the home page pulled up, giant letters filled my computer screen with the words, "Master of Arts in Marriage and Family Counseling." Instead of clicking on it, I immediately closed out of the website. A window had just opened that I did not want to Him to open!

But it was too late. I can still see that window in my mind. I had been so confidently going through each "door and window" God had shown me for a few months because I had promised Him with those exact words. But, I DID NOT WANT TO GO THROUGH THAT WINDOW. That window was not even a viable option. *Shut that window, God!* I stood up, paced around my office, and began to cry. I had a sinking feeling things were about to drastically change and not in the way I perceived as good.

But I had firmly committed to seeing through each opportunity that came up. I had dressed up and gone on interviews for a couple of months. Before that season, I had only been on one interview in my life that didn't result in a job offer, but this time not one interview had led to an open door.

I had practiced saying "yes" and being patiently faithful, but it had been easy so far because I was comfortable with what had been required: get my resume, begin pulling up roots, go on interviews, and wait on the Lord. But, moving to Texas and going to seminary was not something I was comfortable with. This "yes" that He was asking of me seemed crazy.

What's Your Story?

Was there a time in your past when you felt God was calling you to follow Him?

Did you go? Why or why not?

Are you afraid He might be leading you to an uncomfortable step now?

No! Okay, Yes

I don't remember when I finally placed a call to Southwestern, but within a few weeks, I was scheduled for a tour of the school. At 30 years old, a home owner (it was a little house), a Lexus driver (it was a used older model), a grown-up (I paid my own bills), I was going on a seminary school tour. I only told my parents that I was going because I was leaving the state for a weekend. I had watched enough crime dramas on television to know that it was a good idea to tell someone where I was going.

I wanted them to pray for me, but I didn't really want to hear their thoughts. Honestly, I needed to not hear anyone's thoughts, because if anyone petted my desire to not go, I probably would have caved and stayed home. I only wanted to hear God. With no doubt, I had heard Him in my office say "Christian Counseling;" on this trip to Southwestern I had to listen for Him to confirm it.

That proverbial window was difficult to climb through as I drove to Texas, the one state I swore to never live in. I toured Southwestern's campus with a knot in my gut, knowing that I would be making that drive and walking that campus again. Every word confirmed it. This was the window God was opening for me to climb through.

We toured the housing. "We" being me and the bubbly twenty-somethings who were excited to be visiting the campus and to whom I faked friendly as I slowly died to self on the inside. I reminded God of all the reasons why this was not a good fit for me. I was 30. I had never lived in campus housing. I never wanted to live in Texas. How could He expect me to live in campus housing in Texas at 30 years old? I. I. I. Did He not know who *I* was? *I DON'T WANT THIS ANSWER! I DON'T WANT THIS STEP! I DON'T WANT THAT LIFE.*

This whole seminary at 30-years-old scene was not who I am. I am the Ponca City High School Class of '94 Student Council President and Most Likely to Succeed Female Student. I drive a Lexus and go on business trips to New York and L.A. (never mind the Xanax and crying). *What will people think if I go back to school now? Loser. Failure.*

I have a home. I've worked hard for 10 years; am I just supposed to walk away from it all? I can't! I've earned where I am. What will people think? This is not what I wanted. I wanted God to fix the Land I was on or move me to better Land, not take me out into the back woods. I yelled and cried most of the nearly six hours back to Tulsa.

For the next few weeks, or maybe months, I don't completely remember … I grappled. I sweated. I cried. I justified. I doubted. I wrestled (not in a singlet, just emotionally). God was prepping me for another break-through-the-clouds moment.

A friend from Bible Study Fellowship had invited me to First Baptist Tulsa. It was downtown, and I loved the short time I attended there. I shared with a few trusted friends in my Sunday School class what I believed God was calling me to do. One Sunday, a teacher could obviously see my struggle with this calling, probably because I cried during prayer time yet again. I pretty much carry my emotions on my face. Possibly in an effort to alleviate my struggle or possibly to reassure himself in struggles he faced, he told me, "God doesn't care what you do, as long as you do it for Him." I was super not okay with that. He meant well. He was sincere. But, I am convinced now, what I hoped then ... he was wrong.

I knew in my soul, heart, and mind that God was showing me a specific path. I didn't like it, but there it was, and He was leading me to it. God wasn't saying, *Haley, you stay in control of your life. You choose how you will serve me. I think you are really smart, so you guide Me to your plans, and I'll make it happen. I can't wait to see what you come up with, Haley!* Instead, God was saying, "Follow me. This is the direction. I AM the plan maker. Trust me. Is it yes or no?" So I said, "Okay, yes."

That is how it plays out in His Word. For each character in Scripture, God had a specific plan. The only choice was to <u>obey</u> His leading or <u>not</u>. The choice was not to decide whatever plans they wanted to make and just give God the glory. The choice for Abraham, Moses, David, Mary, Peter, and Paul was the same choice for me (and you): yes or no.

This doesn't mean I believe God has a plan for which pair of jeans I should put on in the morning. It just means I believe Him when He says He has plans for my life.

His plans never go against His Word, and it is never too late to seek Him for His plans in your life and family. His plans for me changed my whole life and all the circumstances around me. His plans for you may not change any of your circumstances specifically, but they will change your life, possibly without moving you an inch.

With the grueling decision made, I drove home to Ponca City to tell my parents what I knew was the next step for me. I was going

"The only choice was to obey His leading or not."

to say yes. I didn't understand it; it seemed crazy to me, but I was fully convinced this was His leading.

Honestly, this plan was not what they wanted for me, either. None of that was the vision any of us had for me, or anywhere near what we had been praying for me. They would have never said it or made me feel this way, but they may have been a little embarrassed, too. What does it say about them to have a weirdo daughter? (my feelings, not their words) *Wouldn't it be easier, God, to just give me a kind, good, providing husband and let me fade into the sweet and peaceful life I imagined?*

Land, God! Land is what I prayed for. Land is what my parents had prayed for me. We hadn't been praying for closeness to God; we had been asking for His tangible blessings for me. Anything short of that seemed like failure still. Plan B. Like the back-up plan for a life not going so well.

Through some tears (me and Mom again) and lots of logic talk (me and Dad), they supported me, even in what none of us fully understood. We cried, and I fully committed. Set like flint.

As I drove back to Tulsa following a thunderstorm that had been moving across Oklahoma that day, I cried as I counted seven rainbows that popped up across that Sky over my nearly two-hour drive. Seven. Not four. Not nine. Seven rainbows in that Sky. God's perfect number. God is faithful.

> I would sell my home,
> quit my job of 10 years,
> move to Fort Worth, Texas,
> go to seminary,
> and follow God.

> I was all peace and puke.

What's Your Story?

Has there been a time when you fully surrendered something or someone to the Lord? How did you feel about it?

What ways did God confirm His direction for you?

With whom have you shared your story about His faithfulness?

I've Got This

God's plans for us will not go against His character. For example, He wouldn't specifically call you to steal, cheat, lie, leave your kids, and disregard your spouse to follow Him. We sometimes do some of those things though when we lean on our own understanding to move forward, or when we are actually just trying to escape something and use God as our excuse. The devil subtly distorts the message just enough to have us try and take matters into our own hands instead of fully trusting God. After firmly committing my life to the Lord, the first thing I did was lie. The month was August, school started in January, and I had to figure out how to make all of this happen.

I had worked for the company I was with for almost 10 years, and I thought (my own understanding) that they would fire me immediately if I told them I would be leaving after the first of the year. I needed to sell my house, and I needed my paycheck through the end of the year to make it. And, if I waited until after January 1st, I would get five weeks of vacation pay to start off on a good foot at seminary. I had worked there for 10 years. It was compensation I had earned, I reasoned.

I kept my move from them. All of them. Friends I had worked with every day for nearly 10 years. The friends who had walked down into the cave with me had no idea what I was about to do. I never even told them I put my house on the market. It sold in four days, and within 30 days I moved in with my Grandma Bonnie who lived an hour away, and I told no one.

I never arrived to work before 9:00 a.m. anyway so I was able to maintain that schedule. But, when I started leaving at 4:30 p.m. sharp, they maybe could have suspected something. Grandma was used to having her dinner about the time I was leaving Tulsa, but she began to wait on me for her evening meal. She was even gracious enough to fill my plate for me. As I careened into her driveway on two wheels, I usually didn't even unload my stuff because I knew she would be waiting. I would hustle straight to my seat across from hers, plate filled and milk in glass. I didn't get to say, "No, thanks" to Brussel sprouts because they were on my plate already. She and I shared a lot of coffee on the porch, tears, and laughs before I headed out on this new life. It was such a gift to have those months with Grandma.

I took into my own hands how my leaving had to happen. He gave me a plan, and I was going to figure out the rest. *I've got this, God. Thanks for the agenda. I'll determine how we do this now.* I didn't make any of those logistics decisions because God was guiding me to be discreet or because I was getting wise faithful advice. I did all of this on my thinking out of fear and control. Being discreet as I applied for other jobs, selling my home, or working until the end of the year were not in and of themselves wrong. It was my heart in those decisions that was wrong.

In taking charge of the process, I did not seek God's way and keep my integrity intact. I didn't wait to see how He would handle the situation, to see how my bosses and friends might have been supportive instead of firing or rejecting me on the spot. I'll never know, but I do know my actions destroyed friendships. My actions were seen as calculating and deceptive instead of wise and organized. Based on previous experiences some of my friends had, I was just another lying, manipulative Christian. They were right. What I thought were wise decisions had damaged the way I reflected Christ's character to them.

I regret to this day how I handled that. Sadly, I didn't even fully realize or feel convicted of that until years later. I truly thought that was what I had to do. They may have fired me right away, but maybe I would have seen God work in a miraculous way. I had decided to follow Him, but learning to let Him lead was still a long way down the road.

＊　＊　＊

"I had decided to follow Him, but learning to let Him lead was still a long way down the road."

＊　＊　＊

What's Your Story?

Have you ever done a right thing the wrong way?

Are there decisions you have made leaning on your own understanding instead of trusting God? What were your consequences?

Is there anything that should be done about it now?

Haley L. Scully

Part 2:
Rebuilding

Haley L. Scully

One Jean Skirt and an Empty Quiver

Next stop: Seminary Hill, Fort Worth, TX. A single woman in her 30's was not the status quo at Southwestern Baptist Theological Seminary. To borrow imagery from Einstein ... like a fish walking on dry Land, I walked on that campus. To the fish, walking on dry Land is a miracle. To everyone else, it's just odd looking and maybe a bit scary. Based on the responses of some people, I did not give off the appearance of a godly woman. I was unmarried and had no children in my quiver when there should have been at least five. (Read Psalm 127:3-5 for reference.)

I believe there were those on campus who thought it would have been sinful to speak to me because they wouldn't even. I often felt shame and rejection and anger. Without question, wives were held in high regard, and if you weren't one of them ... then you should have been. I cannot type that without crying. The enemy of my soul kept my eyes peeled for those who ignored or rejected me, and the Spirit in me kept redirecting my eyes to those who accepted and encouraged me. Both were very present at Southwestern, as I'm sure is the case most anywhere.

My love for and submission to Christ didn't appear to hold much weight because I didn't fit the narrative of a blessed woman that was so often preached. The thing is I don't disagree that a woman who is a wife and mother is highly blessed. I am just one example of that narrative not being the only one that God uses. The enemy was telling them and me lies about who I am, and many of us fell to the temptation to believe that what God was doing in me was not enough. It seemed as if my victories in Christ were still viewed as failures. I very much didn't want to be a fish, but the Lord only gave me gills as He prepared me for wings.

I was praying for a husband to cook dinner for and be that Proverbs 31 woman who would honor him. I so badly wanted to be traditionally, culturally, and denominationally more appropriate for a woman of my age – that was the life story I thought was the evidence of God's blessing. But no road I followed Him down in Fort Worth, or anywhere else so far, has taken me to that Land in my own life. I do not think that getting married for the sake of others regarding me as valuable would ever be God's intention for me. He has already assigned me value through Jesus. Frankly, I know that with my head, but, even being convinced that is true, I often have to remind my heart. God has always had a way of making His intentions for me known. Marriage has not been required for me to fulfill my purpose in Him. If someday that is part of my life, I know now that my purpose will not change; it will only be shared.

I am willing to confess the possibility that through my own hurt and disappointment, their rejection and dismissal was magnified. However, my complicit view of myself does not lessen the responsibility, or the impact of their rejection, as men called to be my spiritual leaders. They were not looking for Christ in me; they were looking for their own reflection.

It wasn't until much later that I realized they saw me in much the same way as I saw myself. They were actually my mirror reflection. I felt that women chosen as wives were better, more loved by God, and more valuable than me. I did not view my relationship with Christ as enough evidence of my worth. I blamed God for their looks of disapproval because I very much disapproved of me also as I believed the same wrong narrative. Why didn't He change things? Why didn't He make me who they wanted me to be? Or, why didn't He help them see the me He had called me to be?

Even worse, I began to look at them the way I accused them of looking at me: with self-righteous disapproval. I don't know what it would have taken for me to accept those who rejected me. I didn't feel mercy and grace toward them. In my disapproval of them, I became them. None of us looked at each other through God's eyes.

I hope that this small bit of conversation may lead some to examine their expectations of what it looks like to be a follower of Christ. I pray God shows them, as He often has to show me, if they have tried to conform people to their own image, to a denominational image, or to Christ's image. I've learned through my counseling experiences and education that many times we don't take time to self-evaluate; we only get defensive. When we do that in the Church, we wound one another; and regrettably, I threw as many arrows with my own eyes and heart as ones thrown that pierced me.

Not every pair of eyes on the campus looked passed me. There were professors and friends who could value me beyond my marital status and ragged healing-in-progress appearance. They showed such love and care. They encouraged me and allowed me to serve the Lord in our counseling program and in youth ministry programs on campus. They helped encourage Christ in me. They supported and allowed me to serve God, even alongside other brothers in Christ, and even though I wasn't cooking dinner for a husband.

The professors, pastors, and friends who did care for me displayed that care by speaking as we passed each other down the hall. They would offer invitations for meals in their homes and encourage me to seek the Lord's will for my life ... not just the Lord's husband for my life. Because of them, I began to feel valued and believe that God valued me too. Maybe being single was not His punishment or His neglect, but, at the time, it was His plan. If He gives me all that I need, then maybe I have all that I need.

Seminary Hill was a battle ground in my life. Following Christ was a hill I had decided to die on, and, on Seminary Hill, I fought my will over God's will in attitude, action, and heart. Pride was the big casualty.

•   •   •

"If He gives me all that I need, then maybe I have all that I need."

•   •   •

Previously, I had found my value in accomplishments, leadership, and others' opinions of me. In Fort Worth, I learned to lay it all down.

My Lexus had become a used Suzuki.

My own home had become seminary housing with a rancid possum living under it.

My wardrobe had become, literally, one jean skirt.

My important position in a company had become two part-time jobs just to pay bills.

The second part-time job I took on was, to me in my ignorance, the epitome of hitting rock bottom. I was 31 years old, working in a pizza place wearing horribly unflattering khaki pants, smelling like pizza, and taking my turn cleaning the toilets ... and I was by far the worst employee there. I had never worked food service in my life.

Lia, the young woman who co-owned the pizza place, was a former seminary graduate who saw that pizza place as her ministry ground, and she was amazing. She loved the young employees who were struggling to find themselves as she longed to help them find the Lord. I think she was being extra kind when she hired me. I needed the job, but still, somehow I believed I would be such a bonus for them. I was not.

Not only in attitude, but also in ability, I was not a good employee. I was good at customer service and a smile, but I half-heartedly did the cleaning and was unskilled at food prep, and they all knew it.

A few of the employees were very kind to me and patiently showed me the ropes, but one 17-year-old girl openly hated me. "You laugh like a rich, white girl," she told me one time through narrowed eyes. She would say things just to upset me: "Haley, I'm so hungover," and "Haley, how do I know if I'm pregnant?" To my shame, I looked at her with disdain and not love. I wish I could go back and do that over. I wish I could go back and show her Jesus instead of Haley. *God, forgive me.*

I remember one particularly difficult night after working three shifts – the morning shift at the pizza place, then smelling like pizza going to work the afternoon shift as a bank teller, then back to work the evening shift at the pizza place – I walked out at the close of that evening shift having just cleaned grody toilets, got in my car, and screamed my head off.

Through hot tears, I began listing to God all the things I had given up to follow Him, all the ways He should be blessing me for the sacrifices I had made, and how unfair I thought it was to have to wear horribly unflattering khakis (I know I already mentioned the khakis, but they really hurt my feelings) and cleaning toilets with 17 year olds who hated my guts and were way better at their jobs than me. *What in the world?!* As I dumped it all out, I heard Him in my spirit say, "Why do you think you are too good for this? What makes you better than her that she should clean the toilets and you shouldn't?"

I had felt like that pizza job was either God's neglect or His punishment for my pride, but, after that night, I began to understand that it wasn't neglect or punishment. None of it was. Not the rejection on campus or the pizza sauce on those khaki pants. Christ had already physically took on my punishment for my arrogance. That is literally what He did on the Cross. Those struggles were to set me free of the bondage of my pride and discouragement. I was not paying the price of my sins, I was paying the cost of change.

I was only able to see this was good because I was seeking to grow my relationship with Jesus. If I hadn't been getting to know Him better, then it would have just looked like He was mean and life was harder than it was before I started to follow Him. But, because He was patient with me, and He came and got me even in my hard-hearted state in Tulsa, I could eventually (after the screaming fit) understand that these difficulties weren't punishment (for earlier disobedience, for not being a wife, or for my pride); these struggles were my personal redemption.

"I was not paying the price of my sins, I was paying the cost of change."

These painful circumstances were about freedom and abundance in this life. The Cross does both (John 10). That moment as a child in the front seat of the Cadillac when I stood in agreement with what happened on the Cross was the moment I would no longer suffer condemnation from my sins, but I did begin suffering the pains of redemption (the action of saving or being saved from sin, error, or evil).

I had to decide that the pains of being set free were of greater value to me than the pains of holding on to the Land I tried to demand, the anger, the image, or the pride. Every one of us has to make that decision at some point for ourselves.

That miserable-to-me job and those miserable moments on campus were His grace. Christ freed me of being controlled by them by taking me through them because He loves me and created me for a purpose that required being set free.

It's not that I'm special but because He is. He loves you, too. You can fight it and disagree with it. You can hold on to your position, image, or pride, but it doesn't change who He is. It just keeps you from changing. I've been there.

Freedom can't fully be done through logic and figuring it out. At least for me, it had to be done through experience. He had to mold me, and He took time to do it. I can't type this without crying either. Being healed doesn't happen without the time of healing. The enemy will forever whisper that God is unfair, unfaithful, and mean for punishing us when we are trying so hard.

But the forever and eternal truth is that when we reach up our hand to Him, God pulls out all the stops to set us free. He pulled out all the stops to set me free. That can be really painful, but after those stops are gone and the stagnant air of the hovering storm moves on, the rushing wind of fresh blue Sky fills the space around us, and there is no way we would go back to what was before. The campus became easier to walk across and the toilets easier to clean.

What's Your Story?

Have you ever been disappointed by church leadership? Has that grown bitterness and self-righteousness, or forgiveness and grace in you?

Have you been confused between the difference in punishment and being set free? What was the circumstance?

Are you afraid of the price of change in your life? How so?

Lady Birds and Honey

"But He would feed you with the finest of the wheat, and with honey from the rock I would satisfy you." (Psalm 81:16, ESV)

God gave all the wheat I needed while I was living and learning difficult and gracious lessons in Fort Worth. But, it wasn't all hard. He also gave honey, just as He had promised one late night in Tulsa as I surrendered to His calling.

Flashback: It was the same day as that big discussion when my Sunday School teacher said I didn't need to go to seminary – that I could choose where to serve God. After that conversation I went home mad and sick and confused, but by the end of that night, I was face down on the floor crying and saying yes to the Lord.

I had shared with my friend, Karen, how discouraged I was by what our teacher said to me. I had gone to bed early, pouting, but woke up to the sound of that friend's text message. She told me to turn my TV to Dr. Charles Stanley, that he was talking about what we had discussed that day. I got out of bed to quickly tune in and listen because I desperately needed an answer to my fear that I was making a mistake and would be miserable the rest of my life for it.

Dr. Stanley was talking about following God's calling, and he shared Psalm 81:16. I knew this word was for me on that night. If I would only listen to God and follow His ways, He would feed me with wheat. And, not only feed me, but satisfy me with honey. He was saying in essence that He would take care of me and it would be sweet.

In a supernatural way by the end of Dr. Stanley's message, in my dark living room with only the glow of the TV and my little flip phone's screen, God confirmed this was Him and His plan. I attempted to text my friend back to thank her, but no matter what I entered into my phone's keyboard, at first, only the name God would show on my screen. I hit back space twice to start over and it repeated "God." I was shaking and thinking I was going crazy. I back spaced and began to try my text again. Instead of what I was typing and instead of the name "God," the word "honey" appeared on my phone's screen. I gave up on my thank you text to Karen and went prostrate on the floor.

You may be saying, *Did she just write that God text messaged her?* I did. If you know me personally, you know how hard I try to be logical, and practical, and reasonable. I don't even understand it fully myself. I could not, and still cannot, recreate it or remember exactly what I was texting to make it work. I just know it happened, and by the time I got up from that floor that night I was done wondering if I was making a mistake or not. My life has to speak as the evidence more than any words I could use to explain. I am not who I was because of what He has done.

The honey God promised began flowing in a home in Fort Worth that I moved into with four roommates. We named our home Lady Bird Manor. I had met another 30-something woman who walked away from her career in law to follow God's call to seminary and basically forced her to be my friend. I was a semester ahead of her and badly wanted to help her not feel some of the hurts and disappointments I had felt after arriving. I validated each new phase of reality as she experienced life at seminary, and we joke now how I would say to her, "Kimbrown (I always say her first and last name together), I know how you are feeling ..."

Because I did know. I didn't have to persuade her to feel like I did. The devil doesn't have many tricks. He used many of the same ones on her as he had used on me. I didn't have all the answers, but I wanted to have them all for her. Our friendship was forged in some fires.

She had connected with another girl in our counseling program, MariAnne, who had another friend from college, Sarah, living in Fort Worth. We all needed help to survive financially. *Could I really live with three other grown women?* I tried living with friends in college, and it just about destroyed me. My cousin, Riann, and Lizzy, one of my lifelong friends, had lived with me at different times since those college years, and we got along great. But, the enemy kept pointing me back to one of the most painful times in my life from those early college years. *You can't live with other people. This will go horribly bad.* And on and on and on. But, I really didn't have a choice.

Kim Brown had driven by a sweet little house for rent, and it looked like it could work. We all checked it out. I boldly asked if I could have the master bedroom (because I wanted a room big enough to keep separate if I needed to, as I assumed we would start fighting and hate each other). They agreed. I was the oldest and had the most stuff and probably had my serious face and voice when I asked. I was a bit clenched up inside, but I needed this financially.

The move-in date was set, and again, God set me free. Free of the fear of living life with others, thanks to His grace in giving us each other to walk those couple of years together. He is a Redeemer, and He set me free of the fear that things would always turn out like they had before. Here is a glimpse into life at Lady Bird Manor. I wrote this shortly after we all moved out. The sweetness of the honey the Lord gave us there continues to grow with these friends.

Unplanned – July 28, 2011

From January 2008 through February 2011, I lived in Fort Worth, TX. It's not that I necessarily had anything against Texas, but never in my life did I plan on living here. I seem to do a lot of things I never planned on doing. People have asked me why I left my job and returned to school. It seemed crazy to some; to others, I finally looked like myself for the first time in a long time. It was both the hardest and easiest personal decision I've ever made. Both chaos and peace. I haven't tried to write about that time. I probably will at some point. But this is not that story ...

This story is about a home named Lady Bird Manor, in honor of the former First Lady from Texas: Lady Bird Johnson. I like to name the homes I live in. At first, Lady Bird was home to me, Kim, Sarah, and MariAnne. When Miss MariAnne became a Mrs., Krissie moved in. When Miss Krissie became a Mrs., Kayla moved in. When I graduated and moved out this past February, Allison took my place. Soon after our original move-in date, we thought it would be fun to have a photo shoot to decorate our new home. Not one of these were ever framed or hung on our walls there, but here is the result – first generation Lady Birds: Kim, MariAnne, Sarah, me.

Naming the house ended up helping us bond. We weren't just roommates, we were *Lady Birds*. That's kind of silly, but life is too short to not have some silly. As of tomorrow (forgive me for the following cheesy phrase), all the Lady Birds will have flown the coop.

We considered setting Lady Bird on fire, thinking it might be better to watch her burn than to let someone else move in and not know how truly wonderful of a home she is. But since none of us are certifiably insane, and we are too busy to go to prison, we have decided to just gracefully let her go; praying God blesses the next tenants as much as He did us in our time living there. We hope they appreciate her and have enough furniture to take full advantage of her spacious floor plan.

Our home on South Dr. in Fort Worth, TX had a lot of old school style. Some fancy wallpaper, central speaker system throughout, wood-burning fireplace, working trash compactor, some indoor ironwork, and a beautiful sanctuary of a backyard. In the 60's, Lady Bird Manor would have been high class – like Lady Bird Johnson in her day.

For some reason, it was just more fun to not just "go home," but to go home to Lady Bird. It was more inviting to ask friends over for game night or to a cookout at Lady Bird; to put on invitations for birthdays, going away and holiday parties: "Location: Lady Bird Manor." When Lady Bird's living room was a mess, geckos were climbing her walls and taking showers with us, water flooding her floors, her air-conditioner running non-stop, her grass too high, her fence falling down, ginormous possums roaming her backyard, or mice roaming her pantry, we could scold her, and not each other. "Lady Bird, your grass needs mowed," or "Lady Bird, your kitchen is a mess."

At Lady Bird, "night-night" time was observed at a decent hour. Rainy Sunday afternoons were spent on the back patio with books and coffee and Jesus. There was a lot of coffee and Jesus. At Lady Bird, if you didn't pay rent, you didn't park in the driveway. At Lady Bird, you could say out loud what was bottled up inside. Lady Bird's bushes were lovingly (and aggressively) trimmed, and her varieties of flowers bloomed year-round thanks to Mr. Hernandez who built the house and designed her landscape.

Lady Bird had twinkle lights that made the back yard magical at night but added delight to the daytime just as often. Friends came to take Sunday afternoon naps at Lady Bird and curl up on one of her four couches under one of her many blankets. While preparing a meal, one had more than adequate lighting in Lady Bird's kitchen. Lady Bird hosted a ladies' Bible study each Tuesday night. Lady Bird had her doorways anointed with oil and covered with prayer. Lady Bird's favorite movie was "Anne of Green Gables." Lady Bird loved a good game night, and karaoke always included "Son of a Preacher Man" and ended with "Drops of Jupiter" to mellow it all out.

At Lady Bird, slippers were in style, preferably pink. Lady Bird liked to play her music loudly, especially African worship music and Motown. Bath time at Lady Bird was a choreographed routine and serious business. Lady Bird had delicious chocolate chip cookies and really good bean dip, and her favorite ring tone went like this ...

"You are my strong tower ..."

Lady Bird hosted study groups and showers, planned weddings and life after seminary. Lady Bird showed a lot of grace for our moments of crazy – like the time I walked all the way to my room in the dark, angry that my car key clicker wasn't turning the lights on (school can be hard on a person). Fires were built, tears were shed, exclamations were exclaimed, papers were written, walls were brought down, hearts were strengthened, laughs were laughed, and love was shared at Lady Bird Manor.

I love you Lady Birds, and every friend who played with us, prayed with us, cried with us, ate with us, laughed with us, sang with us and shared not only Lady Bird Manor with us, but some of my favorite moments ever. Moments I never even planned on.

"You make known to me the path of life; in Your presence there is fullness of joy; at Your right hand are pleasures forevermore." (Psalm 16:11, ESV) – *Gracefully Frank*

I had been trying so hard to find solid ground that I valued. I still expected God to open up His blessing in the way I recognized. *Ok, I've followed you. Now give me exactly what I wanted.*

My feet were not dug into Fort Worth mostly because I was tiptoeing around so I wouldn't grow roots where I didn't want to stay. But, as I tiptoed to Lady Bird, roots took hold. Not the kind of roots that bound me to Fort Worth, but the kind of roots that have bound me to these friends for life. Sappy? Honey does that.

Seminary had looked like all Sky and no Land to me. I didn't find a tangible place or specific directions there. I was still uncertain of the job or future God had planned. Instead of clarity or finally being able to piece together all of the puzzle pieces I had been holding in my hand, they all kept floating away.

Instead of giving me a vision of the Landscape I thought those pieces would create, God kept lifting me up out of the picture again and again.

Instead of feeling my feet plant, I began to feel my wings grow.

What's Your Story?

Has God been faithful to you in ways different than you expected?

Have you ever believed a lie that overgeneralizes people or circumstances? "It didn't work out then, it won't work out now." "All men are the same." "People don't change."

Is there a lie you are believing today that is motivating you to say either yes or no to a person, circumstance, or needed change in your life?

More Windows

Most everyone, most always, has advice. I heard a lot of advice as my last year in Seminary was coming to a close. Some said: "You should be sending out a ton of resumes." Others said: "You should not send out any resumes and just let God send the jobs to you." Which one of these suggestions is the right thing to do? Which one is faithful? Which one of those is lazy? Which one over-spiritual? Which one not spiritual enough?

I wondered, *If I send out resumes, is God going to be mad that I did not trust Him to send His job to me? If I don't send out resumes, will I miss the opportunity God has for me because I didn't try?*

Here is what I've settled on … people get excited when they see God work. We like to tell the story. We want to encourage others. But we sometimes get caught up in the <u>way God worked</u> instead of being excited about the <u>fact that God worked</u>. People want to tell their story and encourage others to take the steps they've taken because that is the way God worked for them. But, His thoughts are not our thoughts, and my steps are not your steps. The answers are not the consistent part of the story because we do not all have the same lives, hearts, and plans. GOD is the consistent part.

The good that comes from a testimony is the encouragement to seek God for your own steps – not to try to strap on someone else's shoes, abilities,

"Don't wear other people's shoes or jump on their wagons ..."

or purpose. He will lead you. He has a plan for you that is unique to you. Don't wear other people's shoes or jump on their wagons when God wants to build a wagon for you with a customized license plate. He will build your wagon and then show you where to hitch it.

The goal of sharing my story is not to get anyone to leave their job, go to seminary, and live with a bunch of Lady Birds. I'm sharing the story that God has been writing in me because He has done the work He promised to do in incredible ways.

Start talking to Him. Find a church that leads you to be in His Word, not just pumps you up for the week ahead. Join a gym or a painting class if you want an hour of inspiration a week. Join a country club, a book club, or the Junior League if you want people to hang out with and do some good. But if you want to know better the purpose for your creation, join God your Creator in His church where His Word is being taught and His Spirit is at work.

Don't do it because you have to or because your parents will be disappointed in you if you don't but because something in you wants to know. Something in you knows there is more.

Then listen. Listen for principles that you find in God's Word ... and follow them. Seek Him and nurture your relationship with Him to know Him better. Spend time with Him. Wrestle if you have to, cry if you need to, but do it, even if it seems crazy. Trust Him. Let Him lead you to your leaps of faith, don't decide your own leaps, and don't be led to someone else's leap. He knows your name. He knows the plans He has for you. And those plans look just like you and fit your abilities and strengths.

If you catch yourself encouraging someone to do exactly what you did because that is how God worked in your life … check it. Encourage them to seek God the One who worked in you. His plan for them may be different than yours. The windows that open for them will more than likely be different than the ones He opened for you.

When it came job-finding time for me, I didn't have time or strength to send out a ton of resumes. I was working full time and trying to finish a full load to graduate and keep my sanity. Since I cannot add more hours to the day and after 11 p.m. (and by 11 p.m., I mean about 9:30 p.m.) I am incoherent, I didn't send out resumes. I prayed God would forgive me if I was wrong and still lead me where He wanted me, but all bandwidth I had was just getting me through the moment without the strength or understanding to get me through tomorrow.

As it turned out, connections that had been made while doing what He called me to each day led to an e-mail from one of the counselors I had met while in student leadership on campus. He wanted to let me know a position at their offices in Plano was open, and he invited me to apply for it. He meant Plano, Texas. Not Plano, Oklahoma. There isn't even a Plano, OK. (I Googled it.)

My heart leapt because I so completely respected and admired the ministry in Plano, and my heart sank because it was in Texas. Leaping and sinking make me sick to my stomach. Around the same time, I began talking with a church in Oklahoma that I had hoped might be the place where God would lead me to serve. They were considering a possible Counseling/Singles ministry position that would be new for their church. It sounded like something made for me, and, in Oklahoma!

I began to pray. One position made perfect sense and was kind of the vision in my head of the Land I wanted after seminary. The ministry in Texas was cool but made a lot less sense because I had specifically prayed God would not make me stay in Texas. *(Does He even hear my specific prayers?)* By the way, I hope I don't lose you if you are from Texas. We can both love Jesus, and you be wrong about which state is better.

There was a lot of churning in my head and heart as these two possibilities lay before me. One night I sat down at my little table in my bedroom at Lady Bird Manor, turned on my little lamp, and opened my big Bible. It's the kind of Bible with a big case that needs a zipper. It's the one I bought when I started getting down to the get down with the Lord years before in Tulsa. It's my tank, my foxhole, my safe place.

It's where I keep important things: the programs for the funerals of the people I still miss so much that I'm crying right now as I type this. A bookmark with my sweet niece, Katie's, 3rd or maybe it is her 4th grade picture. There is a thank you note from a pastor who surely has a front row seat in heaven, a list of Scriptures for marriage that Beth Moore handed out when I sat in on a taping of her program (just in case I ever need it). And there is a yellow piece of paper with Scripture on it from a Bible study I did with my Aunt Karla at her house on Leahy Street in Pawhuska, Oklahoma. I drove there each week during her short time of cancer to be in God's word with her and my cousins. I can still remember the moment we needed the paper, and I can visualize my cousin Riann going into Aunt Karla's room and pulling out some yellow card stock from her massive dresser. We wrote Scripture about helping our unbelief on that card stock from that dresser in her room. Now, I'll have it all my days on this earth. It's a special Bible to me. It's the place I return to when I need to go deep.

Back in my room with a fork in the road before me, I opened that Bible up. It wasn't my intention to do an open-my-Bible-at-random-and-do-whatever-it-tells-me-to thing. But, with all sorts of things stuffed in the pages of this Bible, the page I opened to happened to be the page where I had slipped in the business card of the human resources director at the ministry in Plano. I lifted the card up to reveal and read the Scripture it was covering:

"If they had been thinking of the country they had left, they would have had opportunity to return. Instead, they were longing for a better country—a heavenly one. Therefore God is not ashamed to be called their God, for he has prepared a city for them." (Hebrews 11:15-16, NIV)

God had just dropped the mic.

That verse was not written specifically about me, but it was written about God's heart and His character and what He looks for in those who follow Him. In no way does this mean Texas is better than Oklahoma (just to be clear). But, in that moment as I sought the Lord, I realized through this passage that my heart longed for Him more than it longed for home. I closed my Bible and cried for a long time. My will can be broken and made new, but there will be tears.

There was a deep sense of letting go and an even deeper sense of peace. My tears represented sadness that I would not be going home and an indescribable feeling of love and awe for God who again was making His plans for me known. He doesn't have to, but He does. When we seek Him, He will be found by us. He is God of the universe, but so close and so personal. I wish I had never left Him. I wish I could go back and remake some decisions I made that led me away from Him. But in Him, we never have to go back … we always get to go forward in new mercies every morning. This God is worth my every breath.

The next day, or maybe the day after that, I called and left a voicemail for the church leader in Oklahoma to please call me so I could tell them I was not interested in the position. The gracious pastor I had been speaking with called me back a couple of days later after being out of town. He told me things were working out for the best then because they were not going to go forward with the position at that time.

God allowed me that tender moment of surrender with Him at my table in His Word but then also confirmed it for me by even removing the other option. Whatever lay ahead, I will not have to second guess or wonder what might have been. I was staying in Texas. Obviously this was some big Land that He was giving me. Not the Land I had asked for, but it felt like a nice piece of acreage; some good starter Land to plant a few seeds. Even though in my heart Texas still seemed a lot like Sky to me, I was going to get to plant a little bit.

I dug into Texas soil. After three years of tiptoeing around Fort Worth, I began to try to get a feel for the Land with the thought in mind of claiming it. My inner me, trying to be a big grown-up girl, proclaimed quietly to herself: *To this Land, God has brought me, and I shall stay upon it and serve Him!* I didn't want it, but I wanted whatever Land God had for me. And, if that was going to be Texas, then ok. Let's get on with it.

Much like when I first showed up at seminary, I immediately set about finding out why God sent me there. (I like to never learn things and continually repeat old patterns of behavior as if they are fresh, new, and good ideas.) What did it mean? Was this finally where He would reveal the purpose of all the work, all the change, all the stepping out? Maybe He had big plans. Maybe He would let me learn great things and do great things for Him. I set about on probably the most transformative years of my life. For the first time, I was going to have to walk the walk.

Honestly, it was easier to go to seminary. I had been desperate to be back in His will and knew very clearly my life in Tulsa had not been what it should be. I chose to follow God's call to seminary, but also, selfishly at the time, I was running from what felt like a pointless purpose in life.

But after the master's degree, and that three-year ropes course life retreat, I had to <u>live different</u>. Not just have a <u>different life</u>. Class over. There was no try, only do. What I thought had been broken and made new, God began to break more. Seminary had been only the surface.

What's Your Story?

What would you like to have His direction regarding?

What have you done to seek Him for a response?

Who could you talk with about your questions on how to seek God's next steps for you?

Training Wings

Around the time I first left home for seminary, my home church in Ponca City, Northeast Baptist Church, took a trip to Israel. Dad said privately to Mom that going to Israel would be a great graduation gift when I finished seminary. The year before I graduated, Northeast announced another planned trip that would be about three months after my graduation and coincide with my 35th birthday. My parents saw that as our opportunity and signed the three of us up for the trip.

As I planned to accept the position with the ministry in Plano, Mom and Dad presented me with this amazing gift. I would need to ask my future employers if I could take 11 days off, two and a half months into employment. My new bosses were more than gracious in allowing that time. Secretly, my heart was sick. I would have to fly.

I had not flown in almost four years, so I had not addressed that fear. I had just been able to avoid it. Was I going to somehow give in to being afraid and get out of going to Israel? It would be a long flight across a giant ocean, but, it would also be with my parents and people from the church I grew up in. If those weren't the perfect conditions for me to try flying again for the first time in years, I don't know what would have been. There was no reason available to me to say no other than fear.

So, I went to the doctor to get Xanax again. That had helped me back in Tulsa so many years before, and those were only three- and four-hour flights, not 11-hour flights across giant oceans with depths that haunted me. The doctor understood my fear because it was one of his fears, too. His grandparents had been killed in a plane crash. "I'm so sorry for your loss." #helpingnothelping. Nonetheless, with his encouragement and a prescription, I felt prepared to take on that promised Land.

Imagine the moment a flight full of Oklahoma Southern Baptist Baby Boomers and me felt the wheels of their airplane touch down on holy ground. Do you think there were some "Praise the Lord" and "Thank You, Jesus" exclamations, along with a round of applause? There were.

Landing in Israel sparked off 11 days of touring the places we had only read about in the Word of God. From the shore of Galilee, to Bethlehem, to the Mount of Olives, we walked, saw, and breathed in the Land where

Dad, me, and Mom on my 35th birthday in Petra.

God came down in pillars of fire and where He came down into a manger through the Christ child. I circled and dated the pages of my Bible that told the history of places where we stood.

If you can go, go. If going is not in the plans for you, rest well, because Jesus is right next to you. You don't have to go there to know Him, but it is awesome to see.

It was after this trip to Israel, and right before my trip to Austin to visit some of my best friends from seminary, that I began writing my blog, *Gracefully Frank*. The first entry was titled, "Rookie Counselor." I believed the Lord had been showing me some things in my counseling sessions, and I was having swirling thoughts that I unloaded on my counseling supervisor at the ministry where I worked.

He told me I needed to write it and share it. It was an assignment he gave me. I didn't have the option of letting my insecurity about writing keep me from doing it because he assigned me to do it. Writing had been something on my mind for a long time. One of my professors in seminary, Dr. McGuire, told me once that I should be writing. He quickly clarified that he did not mean academic writing (he knew what kind of student I was), just writing-writing. I can still see in my mind the spot where we stood in the counseling offices when he said it. His encouragement meant a lot to me.

So, when my boss told me I should write, I thought about Dr. McGuire's words, and those two mentors whom I respected so much gave me the courage to write and share. This is when my blog became a real thing, and *Gracefully Frank* became an extension of my personal conversations both in my head and out. With my first entry written, I hit send, shut down my computer, and cried my heart out. *What if all the thoughts in my head are just silly? Maybe no one will ever read it. That would be okay. At least I did it*, I thought.

But, a few people did read it, and I didn't die. It didn't change the world or the people in it, but it was that next step of faith in taking the prompting of those around me to do the next thing God had for me. It really wasn't for me to teach the world; it was for God to teach me. If I had been too self-preoccupied and scared of the response, I would have missed or delayed what God was getting ready to do with that little blog. It wasn't for nothing. Something was about to happen.

After my visit to Austin, I decided to write my next entry and just told the story of that trip without having a big lesson on my heart to share. With some of the pressure off of trying to be impactful or validated, I just wrote from the heart and tried adding a few pictures. I love taking pictures. I wrote it, sat back, hit send, and cried again. I am kind of a bawl baby. Sharing my guts is a personal and emotional thing. Each step of trust and obedience began taking me places I didn't expect to go.

Going to Israel and then to Austin were part of a much bigger plan that I didn't realize was unfolding and all connected. All my Land was getting ready to shake, and the Sky was getting ready to open up wide with storms and sunshine and winds and stillness.

Weekend in Austin – June 07, 2011

I have lived in Texas for over three years now, and this weekend, I finally had my first taste of Austin. Weird-cool Austin. This city gets a lot of hype as being a place unlike any other. Music, food, vibe. Willie Nelson lives there. Who is more weird-cool than Willie? I didn't stay with Willie, though. I stayed with Ryan and Jessica Walling, my seminary friends who had become family to me. This was our first time to visit while wearing pajamas. I was surprised to learn they sleep in matching footy pajamas, but it works for them. I loved catching up and talking it all out as we solved world issues. They don't really sleep in matching footy pajamas. I don't have friends that do that.

I told them it would be a miracle if I slept till 8 a.m. on a Saturday but encouraged them to sleep as long as they wanted.

At 9 a.m., I rolled out of bed, proving myself wrong again for the eleventy-billionth time. We went to their favorite breakfast taco dive, and it was really good, but ultimately, I think refried beans shouldn't happen at breakfast. Then we went to some thrift shops and on to SoCo or South Congress Street. It was as billed: weird and cool. I bought a CD off of two guys with a banjo, a guitar, and a harmonica who hadn't seen a shower in days. I haven't stopped listening to their music yet.

Austin was great. Ryan and Jess went to a graduation for one of his students, so I got a little alone time at Starbucks. Then we had dinner and finished with Bananagrams at their house. Ryan won every game in really easy fashion. However, Jessica and I are still cooler than him. Winning Bananagrams doesn't change that.

We spent Sunday morning at the church where Ryan serves as the youth pastor, then had an amazing lunch at Sandra Bullock's restaurant. Between the grits, brick walls, old pictures, chandeliers, and the DJ spinning Motown, you may want to live there. I did.

Finally back on the road again. I stopped in Temple, Texas, to put together a flower arrangement in memory of my great-great-grandfather, whose grave is located in Waco, Texas. He came to America from Ireland and died in Waco in 1896, when my great-grandpa Tom was two years old. I am an ancestry geek. Don't judge. You are probably a geek about something too.

So, go to Austin if you get the chance. Buy a CD off the street, have dinner, stay up late, play games with people who know you really well, and put flowers on the grave of someone who should be remembered.

Thanks to my weird-cool hosts for your friendship and for humoring me when I say "don't move" and then let me take your picture. Everyone should have a Ryan and Jess. – *Gracefully Frank*

Long story short, a little bit more happened than just antique shops, street bands, and cemeteries on this trip. I shared the bigger scope of the story in the next *Gracefully Frank* entry.

So Here Is Something New: I'm Going to Ethiopia In Two Weeks – June 14, 2011

"Oh! The Places You'll Go!" By God's Grace, for me, it looks like that is going to include Ethiopia. Even a week ago, I never would have thought Africa would be on my travel itinerary. Truth be told, I'm kind of a sissy, and Africa seems a little ominous to me. I have admired my friends like Seth and Marianne, and Sarah, and Heidi and

Joel who love Africa and have felt a call on their lives to serve there. Me, I've been thinking about mission opportunities in Ireland. You know, just keeping my eyes open.

However, when you pray "Lord, send me," He gets to choose where, and it is usually where we never dreamed; and the blessing is far beyond our expectations. The last four years of my life are a testimony to that truth. My last blog was about my time in Austin with my friends Ryan and Jessica Walling. Not every blog I write will include them, but at least a few of them will.

Ryan and Jessica are high school sweethearts who have been married for nearly 12 years. For those of you who understand the pain of infertility, you can understand their journey. For those of you who don't understand infertility, just consider one of your biggest heartbreaks … now you can relate. Several years ago Ryan and Jessica began the process of international adoption. God has patiently and persistently led them to adopt in Ethiopia.

Here is where the story for them gets a little bit radical. Ryan and Jessica have committed, after much prayer and confirmation, to adopt a sibling group of four orphans in Ethiopia who have lost both of their parents. I look forward to sharing pictures of these beautiful children ranging in ages from four to 13. Their smiles are breathtaking considering the loss and difficulties these precious hearts have experienced. Others from Ryan and Jessica's adoption agency who have traveled to the orphanage have met these children and are moved by their grace and hopeful hearts. Ryan and Jess are so excited to welcome them into their hearts and home.

After surrendering their desire to give birth to children, and whole-heartedly joining God in His plans for them to adopt these four beautiful kids, Jessica found out she is expecting. Ring the bells!! How often do we hear of God moving this way? They had been told for years that it was a 98% certainty they would never conceive, but now they have been told this is not even a high-risk pregnancy. This baby and the pregnancy are developing perfectly. Ryan and Jessica are experiencing the miracle of a lifetime and the blessing of children in ways only our amazing God could orchestrate. He's kind of a big deal, and Ryan and Jessica trust Him with everything, even with what seems impossible.

So how does that equal me going to Ethiopia? Part of the requirements of Ryan and Jessica adopting their kids is they both have to meet the children before they bring them home. Jessica is due to deliver in October. Bottom line: Jess has to go before she is too far along in her pregnancy to travel, and she also won't be able to travel for months once the baby she is carrying is born. They have been praying for guidance for someone to travel with Jessica, so Ryan, who is a family and youth pastor in Austin, will be able to preserve vacation time and funds to go when they are finally given their date to bring the kids home – hopefully within the next year. As their friend, I have been praying God would work it out for someone to travel with Jess, too.

I never considered maybe that would be me for a couple of reasons: namely, because I'm not a very good airplane passenger. Some of you know this about me. Ethiopia is a long, long way away.

However, I recently flew to Israel and back with Mom and Dad, and thanks to much prayer, I actually enjoyed the flights. I even enjoyed the 11-hour flight to Tel Aviv when I watched some movies, read a little, and pretended I was on a secret government mission. (I like to play pretend. Don't worry about it.)

The other reason I hadn't considered going with her is that I can't imagine how I would afford to do something like this. I only have two days of vacation built up; I am fresh out of grad-school, and don't have a savings built up and I, I, I … I can be ridiculous. I wake up thinking about going, and that thought continues throughout the day. I think I get it, but I can't do this on my own.

So here is the deal: I am asking for help from my friends. If you have just read this, please support what God is clearly and intentionally doing for these five kids: the four who are halfway across the world and the one Jessica is lovingly carrying. Consider helping Ryan and Jessica in their love for the Lord and for these children – Solomon, Rahel, Yoseph, Eyasu, and baby what's its name. I am so blessed by these friends, and by our God who calls me to show love this way (knowing that I will be the one blessed). – *Gracefully Frank*

At the end of that blog post, I humbly asked for people to help pay for the trip. It was a God-sized ask because it is not cheap to fly to Ethiopia with two weeks' notice, and I had zero dollars. My first two donations were from two of my professors at seminary who gave $100 each. It was such a comforting confirmation for me. God was faithful to me through them. He is often faithful to us through one another.

The responses to this blog paid everything, including some of my bills for two weeks off without pay. I gave my friend Casey, whom I lived with at the time, my treadmill in lieu of July's rent payment, and I began to pack for Ethiopia. Because I had been to Israel, Ethiopia didn't seem so inconceivable to me. Jess needed someone, and the Lord opened all remaining doors to make it possible. Because I had already begun my blog just a few weeks before, I had the avenue to ask for help to fund what God had asked me to do next.

Every step of faith led to the next step.

Every step was dependent on the step before.

What's Your Story?

Can you look back and see how one of your steps of faith led to the next opportunity to walk in faith?

Have there been times when you thought you should have taken a step of faith and chose not to? What was the step? Why didn't you take it?

Consider God's eternal perspective of our faithfulness. With mercies new every morning, you never have to go backward. Pray the Lord will bring to mind perceived missed opportunities. Confess them. In Christ, you are already forgiven. Your confession is not for salvation but rather for freedom from regret. Ask Him to show you today's opportunities and give you courage to take your next step of faith.

Next Stop, Mt. Moriah

There are undoubtedly biblical scholars with robes and hats and letters after their name who could detail in much better ways than me the everlasting significance of Mt. Moriah, where Abraham took Isaac to sacrifice him according to God's instruction (Genesis 22). However, I can tell you about my personal Mt. Moriah experience – my own moment of tragedy and triumph. On Mt. Moriah, Abraham went all in with God. He was ready to sacrifice his own son in obedience to God, whom he trusted and loved.

God never <u>tempts</u> us to fall into sin, but the Bible says He does <u>test</u> our faith to rise to His calling. Abraham was given an opportunity to face what could have been his worst fear – losing his son. It would have been Abraham's greatest tragedy to sacrifice Isaac with his own hands. Surely, to consider sacrificing his own son and losing someone he loved so much would make him turn from God and disobey Him.

However, God knew Abraham's heart and the great plans He had for Abraham. He knew that Abraham's faith would have to be refined and pure if he was going to persevere through the battles to come. God gave Abraham the gift of a tragedy to get the moment of triumph. No one, not even Abraham's beloved son, would come between him and the Father. After Abraham's obedience on the mountain, both he and God knew this to be true.

Abraham was all in.

My biggest heartbreak had just happened three years before this trip to Ethiopia when my Aunt Karla Dilbeck passed away of cancer at fifty-five years old. We had lifted her up to God, and He took her home instead of making a way for us to keep her here. I was about to be faced with going through that kind of loss again. I would have to climb that mountain and trust Him with the outcomes again. Would that fear or pain turn me from trusting God?

I'm not Abraham; I don't have a beard. But, the God of Abraham is my God. His mercy, His refining of my faith, and His grace is the same to me. It is the same for us all, but sometimes we have to climb the mountain and exercise our faith and walk out our obedience.

As Jessica and I got up early to catch our flight to Ethiopia, everything went smoothly. I was kind of amazed by the peace that was in my heart as we prepared to board; after all, I had previously prayed very specifically that God would never ask me to go there. Africa signified complete lack of control to me. No one could get to me there. No one could help me there. It was a complete world away from my Grandma's front porch. And yet, I did have peace. I had no idea how life was about to change. I didn't know that in flying to Ethiopia I was climbing Mt. Moriah. But, as I flew across the ocean toward the complete unknown, I enjoyed myself . . .

In-Flight – July 05, 2011

It's 4 a.m. Addis Ababa time. I'm looking out the window at the lights of the cities that dot the coast around the boot of Italy. I seriously just typed that. I've seen that boot on maps, and although my feet haven't touched the earth there, my eyes have seen the lights that outline the sole and tip of that fancy Italian boot. I've just asked for my third little can of ginger ale, and, having turned my in-flight radio to the Andrea Bocelli station, I'm feeling inspired to write. I don't want to forget these moments.

Jess and I are occupying row 39 seats K and L. I'm by the window. I love being by the window. That is a big deal for me, for those of you who know I've been known to lose heart a little prior to flying the past few years. My heart is full today. We are flying on Ethiopian Airlines. I have a pillow, a blanket, one of those silky little eye cover things you see in movies, knee high socks, and a little mini toothbrush with toothpaste. Let's just say my satisfaction is easily bought with little presents. Our flight is filled with Ethiopian people who are gracious and accommodating. We have been greeted with smiles and courtesy every minute of this journey. I find myself wanting to hug people.

The man in front of me is reading a book on market research. One chapter was titled, "What Test Markets Won't Tell You." I cannot imagine why anyone would want to read that book. I respect his choice, and hope he gets what he wants to know from it, but I can't be more serious when I say I would never.

I keep wondering, "How did I get here?" I am really blessed that God continues to make the world a lot smaller for me. I love where I'm from, I appreciate where I've been, and I am totally intrigued and surrendered to where I'm going. When I am so focused on trying to consider what I am getting out of life, I'm discontent, anxious, and frustrated. When I am focused on Christ's life in me and through me, I get to be a part of some pretty amazing moments – like this one as I find myself on a plane high above the earth, sippin' ginger ale, looking at the lights of Italy, and now listening to the new Greg Allman CD "Low Country Blues." Good sound. P.S., I just got to feel baby Walling kick. "It" better not be getting sassy.

What a wonderful, fascinating world. I hope I get to see more of it. What an infinitely wonderful Savior who loves us more than we give Him credit for and way more than we ever show one another. I pray I know Him more every day.

The stars look really close up here, and I just found "Joshua Tree" under the oldies section of the radio. Is that possible? Is this album oldies? It's not. I got this cassette for my 13th birthday, and that was just the other day. I was wearing a Debbie Gibson hat when I opened it. I'm hitting play, and I kind of hope we're not almost there. – *Gracefully Frank*

I had no idea that as I woke up that morning to board the plane and liftoff into the Sky again that my dad woke up unable to walk. For months, he had dealt with what we thought was a strained back. He had a hernia he needed surgery for but was anemic so surgery had been delayed. He had been having a bunch of seemingly unrelated, aggravating, and uncomfortable symptoms of something much larger.

As I was in the air flying to Ethiopia, my mom was calling Johnny McCloud, our friend who is family, to come to the house to carry my dad down the stairs and into the car to rush him to the emergency room in Oklahoma City where my brother Chris waited for them. As I sipped ginger ale in an airplane over the Atlantic Ocean, high in the Sky, the Land below was quaking.

A few hours after setting foot in Africa and getting settled into our Ethiopian home for the next week, we were able to get on Wi-Fi. I had a message from my sister-in-law, Leigh. I don't remember exactly what it said, but it was something to the effect of, "Everything is okay, but your dad was taken to the emergency room and is in the hospital. Call us when you are able."

I read that sitting on a porch in Ethiopia. To say I had a full blown come-apart is an understatement. *I was in Ethiopia! How could God let my world fall apart when I was on the complete other side of it?*

Highly Contrasted Moments – July 05, 2011

We arrived safely in Addis Ababa on time and with no sleep. It was 8 a.m. here, but our bodies were at midnight. The plane to Ethiopia was one of the big planes you would expect it takes to carry you to another continent, but the staircases they wheeled up to the doors for our dismount reminded me of those metal bleachers from high school. They herded us onto buses where we were *packedinthisclose* and began the journey to the terminal. I'd say it was about 30 yards, and certainly did not warrant the gas spent turning the ignition. An elderly lady in heels who must have known how my breath smelled, looked at me and said, "I would have walked that instead of cramming into this bus." Me too, elderly lady, whose breath I knew too well.

Our three checked bags were, if not the last three bags in the baggage claim area, then definitely the second-to-last three bags. But we got them, intact and ready to roll. Our host picked us up and brought us to our guesthouse. He took us to get coffee. Really, really good coffee.

There is an Australian couple staying here in the house, a young lady doing work with women and children here, and a couple who adopted two girls a year ago from Ethiopia and brought them back for a visit. She is from Chicago, a nurse practitioner, and works for Minute Clinic. Jessica is a nurse practitioner and works for Minute Clinic in Austin. Say it with me: "small world." Our host upgraded Jess and I to the master suite with two beds, a sitting area, and a balcony. It is quite lovely.

Meanwhile, back at the ranch ... My dad was admitted to Mercy Hospital in Oklahoma City. I wish there was a way to type that sentence for full understanding, but it isn't possible. He has been in a lot of pain, but now that he is there, he is not in pain. That is good. They are running tests to determine the cause of the pain he has had for the past several months – that we have been thinking was a pulled ligament or infection.

He has been to doctors consistently for several weeks, ruling things out. We are now working to rule out cancer. I type that word as I sit here in Addis Ababa millions of miles away from him. I'm feeling a lot left out of the "we," not being with him, Mom, Chris, and Leigh and our family right now. But, yesterday morning as I was preparing for liftoff in Washington D.C., I felt so at peace and overwhelmed by God's presence. I posted a Facebook status just to put it out there: *"Wherever you lead. Whatever is clear, whatever is confusing. Because of whom you are and faith you've given me, all my love, all my life, Jesus."*

That was a whole continent before I knew Dad was in the hospital. But, in His strength, it is still my status today. Please pray for Dad as we head into this confusing time this week. Pray for results that will lead us to treatment to heal his pain. Pray it is not cancer. Pray I don't lose my mind and hijack a plane to get home to him.

After all that, our host took us to the orphanage, and we met the kids. Solomon, quiet and gentle, keeping an eye on everything while beaming a beautiful smile. Rahel, a little more shy. Her eyes smile first, but her mouth is not too far behind. She speaks less English than her brothers, so she lets them lead. Yoseph likes to take the lead. He is a HUGGER, and he likes to give kisses and hold hands, and he has a beautiful – let me repeat – beautiful singing voice. I'll cry my

eyes out. And Eyasu, the youngest, has an imagination. He wants to hold hands, and he says, "I love you" a lot. Me too, Eyasu.

Seeing Jessica with her kids is one of life's joys. I can hardly wait for the rest of her friends and family to see it too. The kids were right next to her the whole time. She showed them video of Ryan as they were laughing and saying, "Papa." They are going to fit right in with Ryan. All four of the kids sang songs for us, showed us their rooms, held our hands, and showed us such love. I thought it would be the other way around.

I will get down on the floor and bawl, there is so much emotion going on up in here! I have a God who is sufficient, who led me here, and is allowing me to be a part of this time in this place. It is confusing that all of this would have to happen in the same minutes of time, but I have a God who promises He never leaves me nor forsakes me. He never leaves Dad nor forsakes him. He has never left Ryan and Jessica. He never left these children. He works all things for the good of those who He loves and are called according to His purposes (Romans 8:28). That is peace in all circumstances. All my love, all my life, Jesus. – *Gracefully Frank*

God did not make my dad sick for me to have this experience. We are all subject to the fallen state of this life. Cancer happens, and it happened to him. For any of us affected by his cancer, God used this tragedy in our lives to deepen our faith and understanding as we turned *to* Him, instead of away *from* Him.

For me, being eleven million miles away when this initially happened (that distance is probably more emotionally accurate than geographical) gave me that moment on the mountain to decide if I would turn back or keep going forward. Would I trust God and stay where He so clearly called me to be? Or would I try to jump on the next plane and get home to where my heart was with my sick dad and broken-hearted mom?

When I first found out he was in the oncology unit at the hospital, not knowing any of the details but knowing things looked bad, I wondered if Dad would die before I got home. I had several hours to consider my next steps in my own understanding before I could get a clearer picture from my brother back home. When it's "go-time," I usually go. I get things done. I handle and help. This was go-time for <u>my</u> dad and mom. If ever there was a moment when I needed to save someone ... *Oh, yeah, wait. I am not the Savior. I'm not even a doctor.*

I am to be who, what, and where the Savior leads me to be and trust Him with the ones I love the most. I was to be with Jess in Africa for the next week. There was no doubt that God led me to Africa because it certainly wasn't my idea. *My heart is the Lord's, and whom have I in Heaven, or on Earth, but Him?* So I stayed. In my heart and mind, I gave my dad and the prospect of ever seeing him alive again to the Lord. God allowed the moment of tragedy to give me the moment of triumph. In Ethiopia, I walked up the mountain, laid my Isaac on the rock, and truly and forever went all-in with God.

● ● ●

"God allowed the moment of tragedy to give me the moment of triumph."

● ● ●

What's Your Story?

Have you had a moment with God when you were given the opportunity to trust Him, choose Him, and follow Him fully? What happened?

Are you scared of having that moment because you are afraid of what it might cost? Or what you might have to go through?

Have you talked with God about it? Or are you avoiding the conversation?

Mountaintops Are Not Final Destinations

As I type this today, our family is six years past Dad's diagnosis, and I sat by him at dinner last night. We went through two very intense years of treatment, and he continues weekly maintenance to keep cancer from getting a foothold. There have been many tears and praises and blogs and lessons learned through our family's journey with cancer. After all that God has done, even Dad has said he would not go back to who he was before. God has truly been faithful and has continued to work all things for our good.

Dad's diagnosis and cancer battle was an obstacle that very much drew my attention to the Land I sought. In my fear, I wanted to dig in, hold ground, and run to my home Land to tend to the things of this earth. God kept gently pulling up the roots that I desperately wanted to take hold of so that He could keep lifting me up to the plans He had for me.

Each step of faith that I thought would finally get me to the

Land I longed for actually just took me closer to the next ledge from which I was to leap.

The trip to Israel made the trip to Ethiopia possible. The trip to Ethiopia was my moment on the mountain and what I thought was the whole point of all this mess – to bring my heart and will into full surrender to God.

I've arrived at my destination; we've pulled this plane up to the gate. Now, I'm ready to unbuckle and go claim my Land. I've been to the mountain, God was faithful, and I'm all set. Thanks for the ride, God. You were totally right. Now let me snuggle in to the life for which I have prayed. Surely all this preparation has been meant to lead me right where I keep asking You to lead me. Right? You take me through a series of obstacles to refine my heart and then give me everything I have wanted?

But God wasn't preparing me for my plans; He was preparing me for His. I kept thinking we had reached our final destination, but each one of these mountaintops were for preparation. Each mountaintop was also a place where I could have chosen to climb down instead of leap off. I could have decided to be angry when Dad was diagnosed. I could have allowed fear to prevent me from flying.

We always have the choice to choose belief or unbelief, trust or distrust, faith or fear. Thankfully, when the next cliff presented itself, I had seen enough with God in the leap before that He empowered me to let go and jump again.

I went to Israel with Mom and Dad and my home church. God gave me all the people who made me feel safe. Then I went to Ethiopia with Jess because she needed me. God was asking me to help someone else, and I could see the purpose to help my friend whom I loved.

The next leap would be to go alone to India. India, you guys. I never even thought to tell God not to send me there. India was basically Mars to

"God wasn't preparing me for my plans; He was preparing me for His."

me, and it should have been a given that I would never go there. If I didn't want to go to Mexico and Africa, then obviously it's a "no" for India. His plans were starting to get ridiculous.

See what had happened was … I answered the phone when an Indian couple who were in the United States visiting their daughter called the ministry where I worked; they wanted to get resources before returning to India. They had been involved in ministry for many years. Arrangements were made for them to visit our offices, and, since my manager was out the day of their visit, I was told to give them the tour. Just minding my own business. Unsuspecting. Naïve. Thinking I was all settled. I gladly met with them and enjoyed hearing their hearts and showing them around. We were fast friends.

Over the next several months, they sent me their monthly e-newsletter showing how they had used our resources for marriage counseling events they were doing in India. I forwarded their e-mails to the director of our international department so he could see the fruit of the books in their language he had given them as gifts. After several months of seeing what God was doing through this couple in India, our international director replied back to me and asked to have a conversation about their ministry in India. If I had known in advance where that conversation would lead, I am sure I would have run out of the building.

He requested that I ask them if they would be interested in having someone come and explain how the resources from our ministry would help them and other church leaders. Would a training conference be helpful as they try to grow hope in India? Through a series of e-mails, they confirmed it would be helpful. Many pastors and church leaders they contacted were very much interested in being equipped with these resources and tools for counseling help in their churches. (*Of course they were.*)

The ministry we worked for had several Indian languages already translated, and, unbeknownst to me, the international director had been praying for openings to share how our resources could help the Church counsel and disciple one another.

I relayed their response to our international director, and he told me he thought I should be the one to go do the training. *Who, what, now?* My "yes" to God seemed to be getting more costly. Lights kept turning green on these plans, and it was so scary to me. Israel with Mom and Dad and Ethiopia with Jess were fine, but India by myself?

Nope,
nope,
nope.
But, okay, yes (followed by a heavy sigh and tears).

One particularly fear-filled day, I went into the international director's office and cried and cried. "Why am I going? Shouldn't someone else go do this training? Like, a real person who knows how to go to India?" He welled up with tears too and said, "I don't know why. But, when I pray about this, the Lord keeps confirming to send you."

I was sick and scared, but all in. For many, this may seem kind of ridiculous, as going to India may sound like a wonderful adventure, but it did not seem that way to me. Going to India was not who I am. But God had done too much for me to actually say no at that point. I had seen enough to keep saying yes, but it was gut wrenching. India. Alone. Never in all my days.

Each step before led to this step. If God had revealed all His plans to me in the beginning, which is what I tend to beg Him to do, I would not have been able to handle it. But because He shoots messages to me on the as-needed basis, He slowly builds and builds my faith and His power in me. I will not say no to Him. He has done too much to go back now. But sometimes I forget who I am, and I think I am a chicken …

Next Degree of Glory – October 24, 2012

It begins today. I'm going to begin sharing this India journey with you. Two weeks from now, I will do my own proverbial version of jumping off the cliff, Sky diving, trusting. It's funny how I thought moving to Fort Worth would be my big leap in life. But He keeps taking my breath away with new and further leaps. I'm so uninformed of the agenda! The more I try to figure the agenda out, the more anxious I get. The more anxious I get, the more I'm driven to seek Him. The more I seek Him, the less the agenda matters.

Laying aside every weight (*Where is God leading? What is He doing in my life? Is He taking care of me? Will I stay in Texas? Will I move closer to home? Will I ever get married? Will I ever be a mother?* And a whole host of other thoughts for family and friends that I would like to see Him fix and heal), and laying aside every sin (I'm going to opt out of listing those here), I am going to run with endurance the race that is set before me … looking to *Jesus* (Hebrews 12:1-2). He's been softly and tenderly and silently letting me squirm and question and strive, all to bring me to let go again. Let Him lead again. Surrender is always so difficult (my struggle) and sweet with Him (His grace).

Yesterday, I had to have my crying fit. I knew it was coming. Preparing for <u>India</u> – so outside of my preferred box – is a little daunting to me. Daunting equals stress. Stress equals a moment of <u>unabashed</u> tears. My co-workers are so lucky. I didn't go out into the lobby and tear my clothes or throw ash around, but I did the equivalent at my desk with a friend who is a blessing in my life. We talked about God's silence. We talked about how the Holy Spirit is the One who will be at work in India. I just have to let go and let Him do it. Then I sat at my desk, praying for clarity and courage, the same prayer that first led me to Fort Worth. And it began to get clearer, and He is making me feel stronger.

I really wish I was more classy and could report to you that with total coolness I am living this life of surrender to Him. But I am just kind of messy. I wrestle with where He has led and where He is leading. I get insecure and awkward and unsure and angry and sad, and, although I do not lose my resolve, although my faith continues to grow, I do sometimes lose a little heart when my frailty is exposed.

When I ask, "Who am I?" to go, I keep getting reminded to ask, "Who is He?" The answer to "Who is He?" shuts my mouth. Restores my joy. Heals my wounds. Grows my love. Quiets my fears. Directs my footsteps. Washes me clean. Transforms my life. Sets me free. Still makes me cry. I love Him, and love sometimes spills out of my eyes.

"All this is from God, who through Christ reconciled us to himself and gave us the ministry of reconciliation; that is, in Christ, God was reconciling the world to himself, not counting their trespasses against them, and entrusting to us the message of reconciliation. Therefore, we (I) are ambassadors for Christ, God making his appeal through us. We (I) implore you on behalf of Christ, to be reconciled to God. For our sake he made him to be sin who knew no sin, so that in him we might become the righteousness of God." (2 Corinthians 5:18-21, ESV)

So after my little fit yesterday, I got a lot of work done. Then I went home. I listened to "Simon and Garfunkel's Greatest Hits," one of my favorites, had a fun conversation with someone I love (talking about ice cream and good news), cooked dinner, worked on my church home group study that I will go to again this weekend, read a couple of chapters of *Love Does*, and said goodnight to the day.

This morning on my way to work, I accidentally hit "shuffle-all" music on my iPod as I hooked it up in the car. The first song was a Willie Nelson song from his album, "Stardust," another one of my favorites. So I left it on shuffle. As I drove, the next song that came on was Alanis Morrissett's, "Thank You." I have not actually listened to this song in years, and, as I really listened to the lyrics, I began to laugh all the way to work. I don't know what all these words to this song meant to her, but I know what they mean to me. There are so many words from yesterday in those lyrics (see the underlined words above).

Maybe that wasn't a coincidence. *Maybe He shuffled my iPod? Can He not do that?* You could roll your eyes at that, or maybe you might listen for Him a little closer in your life. He's kind of great. He is the God of the universe, and yet, because He is Love, loves me. He takes care of me, from one degree of glory to the next. Ridiculous.

It ruins the mood to just type out the lyrics, but if you want to see them, Google it. Or if you have a second, maybe listen for yourself. For the record, I'm not on any antibiotics. – *Gracefully Frank*

What's Your Story?

Has God ever asked you to do something surprising? Maybe something you didn't want to do, but you did it anyway? What were the results? How long has it been?

Not every thought that passes through our mind or every song that comes on the radio is a message from God. That voice in us from Him must align with His Word. But the more we know His Word and the more we watch for it, the more we hear Him. Have you ever heard God outside the walls of the church? How did it line up with His Word? What did you do? And what were the results?

India

I went to India and back for the next once-in-a-lifetime trip, following Jesus wherever He leads. While doing the work I've been equipped to do, God is constantly at work in me. He is faithful <u>through</u> me to others and <u>to</u> me. The wonderful Indian couple who had become my friends in Dallas, greeted me at the airport with roses. God gave me such a gift in them and their care for me during our service to the Lord.

Rev. Dr. Christopher David and his wife, Hepzi, had hosted many ministry partners over the years through their work with the Billy Graham Association in India. Hepzi always walked a step ahead of me as she took care of me. She let me know what to put on my plate in the buffet line during our training events. "Eat this, not this. This is goat. Do you like goat?" "Uh. Nope." "Okay, don't eat this."

They took me to a lovely Indian department store to give me a gift of traditional Indian clothing for our visit to church on Sunday. She picked out a teal and purple ensemble for me that I proudly wore. She was a blessed mother, sister, and friend to me. My faith grew because of their love and care. God was everywhere.

They asked me to speak for a few minutes at their church on Sunday to explain one of the resources from our ministry that would be provided by their church to their small group leaders. "Sure," I said. I did not know as I casually said "sure" that there were 3,000 members at their church on Sunday mornings. *Did I say yes? I meant nope. Okay, yes.*

I prayed. I reminded God that He was supposed to do through me what He was asking me to do. He did. When I got quiet with Him and in His Word, He led me. He gives me the words to clearly inform and respond. Every time. Not that it goes smoothly every time. Not that sometimes I am not distracted, insecure, and tired, but He is faithful to those He stands me before, and to do what He promised through me, in bringing us together.

Speaking to 3,000 Believers.

View out my hotel window.

This is us in India.

Our time in India coincided with a holiday there that was celebrated by fireworks shot from the rooftops at midnight. I didn't know that was going to happen. When the clock struck twelve and the fireworks launched, I shot up out of my hotel bed as I heard them begin exploding and thought, *Well, this is it. This is where I die. The gunmen sound close.* As I began to consider my escape options, I went to take a slight peak behind the curtains of my upper story window, being careful so whoever was shooting wouldn't be able to see me. I saw that it was not gunmen filling the streets, but rather fireworks filling the Sky across those rooftops. It was literally amazing.

Why do I get to be here, God? Why isn't someone else getting to see all of this? Like someone who really knows what they are doing? Someone with courage, someone with a full quiver, or who looks like they should? Why me?

With peace that passed understanding and bone-deep gratefulness, I watched the firework show through tears. I was beginning to fall in love with the Sky that God was giving me. I long for Land, but I am amazed by the Sky. One time I was in India and watched fireworks light up the nighttime sky over the city rooftops as far as the eye could see. Only God.

My hosts dropped me off at the airport, and I was growing anxious about the long two days of travel home. I was probably still a little overwhelmed by all that God had done during my time there. The veil was torn between me and my fears. But still, I was feeling a little extra alone as I stepped into the airport in the middle of India with a sea of unrecognizable faces. I bought a magnet and some chocolate and went to find my gate.

As I walked toward the seats in the gate waiting area, I saw a red hat with familiar words in all caps and bright white stitching: "SOONERS." I literally yelled across the floor, "I'm from Oklahoma!" Startled, the man under the hat and his friend stood up to greet me as neither hell nor high water would have kept me from getting to their side.

The hat was on the head of a pastor who had been with one of his deacons on mission in India for a couple of weeks. They were from Garland, TX. No joke. His son was a student at The University of Oklahoma, home of the "Sooners." They were beautiful to me, and they were on each of my flights all the way home.

I'm sure I went into way too much detail of what I was doing there, but, after my story, the pastor said words I will never forget: "Well, sis, you're with us now." And, I was. Never were truer words spoken. Like white on rice, all the way home.

> They could have been on any flight.
> He could have worn any hat.
> But, they were on my flight.
> And, he wore that hat.
> *I see you, God.*

India. Check. Again, I thought that would be the last of it. You guys, I have my share of incorrect assumptions.

It is a good thing to begin seeing the fruit of change and the purpose of what God has been doing in our lives, but it can be a little destabilizing. He was leading me to do things that I had specifically prayed against and had honestly thought were not even possible. *Is it even ok for me to go to India by myself and speak in church? Is it even ok for me to teach men and women?* All of this was feeling pretty drastic and a bit traumatic.

There is a passage in Scripture that comes to mind: Luke 13. I'm going to share the King James Version because it sounds fancy:

> "And He was teaching in one of the synagogues on the Sabbath. And, behold, there was a woman which had a spirit of infirmity eighteen years, and was bowed together, and could in no wise lift up herself. And when Jesus saw her, he called her to him, and said unto her, Woman, thou are loosed from thine infirmity. And he laid his hands on her: and immediately she was made straight, and glorified God." (Luke 13:10-13, KJV)

I can relate. I have been emotionally bowed over and unable to lift myself up many times. Fear, insecurity, incorrect assumptions, and wrong beliefs have kept me bound. I had been knotted up in regards to who I was, how ministry in my life and through my life should look. But, God, in Fort Worth, in Israel, in Ethiopia, and in India was pouring oil on those knots, and I was coming loose. I actually never wanted to be loosed. My comfort zone was in those knots that kept me on the ground, in Oklahoma, and in good standing with cultural norms.

Writing helped me think through my wrong beliefs. Where did they begin? What was God showing me now? I wrote the following blog post about a month and a half after returning home from what I thought was the far edge of the world. Not to jump ahead, but I've gone way past that edge now.

Wait, What? – January 05, 2013

When I was in junior high and high school, our youth group attended a youth evangelism conference in Oklahoma every year. I don't know if it still is, but back then, it was held right after Christmas. One year it was in Del City, one year, Moore, I think. I have a lot of great memories with my youth group – worshipping and playing with them. There are a few highlights that stand out from those years in no particular order. Dawson McAllister ate goldfish on stage one time. One of those churches literally had a little river running through it down by the stage. That seemed pretty cool. My high school boyfriend and I both cried as I walked forward with him when he decided to receive Jesus as his Savior. That was certainly a highlight. But it was after my first year attending that I went home truly believing God was going to kill me. Soon.

Here is why: A preacher standing on the other side of that little river delivered a passionate sermon talking about our assurance of going to heaven and asking us to think about who in our lives did we know was not saved and would be spending an eternity in H-E-Double Hockey Sticks.

Were we just going to let that happen? What would we be willing to do for them? Would we give our life like Jesus did, or would we stand by and do nothing? I took him literally and did some deductions: *I know I'm saved. I know Grandpa Corky is not. I'm here for a reason. This must be it. Go time.*

A good friend of mine was also unsure about a family member. We cried, not wanting them to go to Hell. We stood up and walked down front to give our lives for theirs. There were a lot of other kids going down front. I bet some of them were confused too. I didn't know how God would kill me, but I was certain that when I died, Pa would be sad and accept Jesus as his Savior. I remember wondering if I would be in a car wreck. It seemed the most likely. I wasn't sick, and it wasn't tornado season (the only other two causes of death in northern Oklahoma). As a week or so wore on, I grew more anxious waiting for the moment until I ended up in bed crying my eyes out. My mom, having sensed something was off, came in to make me tell her *what in the world was going on!?!?.*

I let her in on my impending death but told her not to fear ... *Pa would be saved.* I don't remember exactly what she said, but in no uncertain terms and with her I'm-going-to-whip-someone's-b-u-t-t voice, she reminded me that Jesus had already died for Pa, and He didn't need me to. She seemed pretty emphatic about that. And I'm not sure she didn't make a phone call or two to make sure others were on the same page.

I had focused on the wrong point of the sermon *(or maybe he had stressed the wrong point of the sermon?)*. I had focused on the surrender of my life instead of rejoicing in the surrender of Christ's life that I could share with Pa. "Tell the good news," not, "Be the sad story that serves as a warning to others." One focus leads to unnecessary despair, the other to truth and assurance. The thing is, sometimes God does take the sad stories and turn them into good. Many times that is when we truly seek Him. In the moments of tragedy beyond our understanding, we seek a higher understanding.

Tragedy is a result of a broken world where cancer, car wrecks, and mad people exist. But it's not the sad story that saves. It's realizing we need to be saved and accepting the gift of salvation that the life, death, and resurrection of Jesus Christ offers. Although many have died to share the good news of salvation, only One needed to die for the plan of salvation. The preacher was passionately calling us to share the gospel, not be the gospel.

The gospel already is.

The gospel is Jesus.

I don't know if that unfortunate misunderstanding at the conference is where

"Although many have died to share the good news of salvation, only One needed to die for the plan of salvation."

my wrong belief started that surrender to God is going to be dreadful and the opposite of anything I ever wanted or if that was already in me. Some people RUN to give their lives to God. I have been patiently, graciously, and thankfully dragged here. I'm not proud of that, but that's the truth. I wish I gave in more easily, as easy as it was in my youth. But I spent some time turned from Him. Now I have to fight for Him in me, but that struggle (according to Romans 5:3-5) produces perseverance, character and hope, and a lot of peace that I didn't have fighting for other things.

If I'm going to fight for something, I want it to be for the hope of mankind. I believe Jesus is our hope. It pains me to think of the times I denied Him or made little of Him, and then to think how He doesn't think of those times. Ugh. As I work out my salvation, each new surrender to His will over my fear, selfishness, doubt, etc. is often

followed by a wince,

followed usually by tears,

followed by a leap,

followed by increased faith,

followed by renewal of my mind,

followed by a transformation in my life,

followed by laughter at the silliness of the wince and tears,

followed by thankfulness,

followed by testimony which you are reading now.

Sometimes I'm wrapped up in the lie that God's will for me isn't what I want. Like moving me to Texas or taking me to India. But He is our Creator. What He created me for is what every fiber of my being wants, even when I don't know what that is or even when my eyes, my heart, my society, and my flesh argue against it based on my own limited understanding. I can focus on what I can see with my eyes and try to make happen what seems normal to me, but that will not lead to fulfillment of my life. Only the Creator can know the purpose of the created, and He wants us to know the steps to take and will show us in His timing when we ask.

The Creator gave us the ability to choose. This is seen throughout the Bible which is filled with examples of people who said, *OK, yes. Your will be done*, or, *You know what? I'm out. I'm going to do something different that makes sense to me or that feels good.*

Doing something different may feel right in our youth, in our flesh, in our country. Both paths lead through trials, joys, relationships, jobs, conversations, achievements. But each path, although they end the same way, has a very different outcome and very different lasting impacts on the generations that come after us.

We are never too far down one path that we can't pick up the other, and, unfortunately, we are never too far down one path that we can't be tempted by the other. That is life. We can look for God, or we can ignore Him. We can grow in faith in Him, or we can grow in denial of Him. We say "yes" or "no" based on what we believe about Him. And what we believe about Him depends on who we are listening to ...

Case In Point

In the very first book of the Bible, Genesis, Eve believed the lie that by doing what God wanted her to do, she would be missing out. She could choose to obey, not eat the fruit, and be an obedient sucker according to the snake, or she could take the fruit by the horns and get out of life what she believed would be more than what God was offering. *Eat up and ride out, Eve! What does God know about you? Does He even care? Are you being a fool by not partaking? Is He even trustworthy?* (Those words are not in Scripture. I'm just fleshing out a little bit what the temptation looked like in my mind and how that temptation sounds when the snake says it to me.)

It would have been okay for Eve to run to God (whom she walked with and fellowshipped with and knew personally) and say, *God, I am being tempted to eat the fruit by a snake I just met! He says YOU are holding out on me. Is that true? What in the world is going on?!*

But Eve chose to act on her questions instead of ask them. She didn't even say, *Hey, snake, meet me back here in a week. I'm going to think about it.* She acted on the deception instead of acting on what she had known to be the truth: that God is good.

Action is what got her into trouble, and she got what she asked for: she had knowledge of good and evil – stepping out from the shelter of one and exposing herself to the other. And since knowledge can't be

> "...Eve chose to act on her questions instead of ask them."

undone … we are all paying the consequences and acting just like her.

Acting on temptation is much easier than asking questions. It's mindless; we don't have to think about it – we just do. It doesn't take perseverance or character. It's just satisfaction in the moment. We just bite the fruit because we hear someone tell us we are being manipulated, without considering that those words are falling out of a mouth determined to kill us. For Eve, Paradise was lost because of believing the true manipulator. What have you lost? I know I've lost more than I should have.

Is God Good?

A few weeks ago, a sermon at church from a pastor who loves the Lord and his congregation hit me between the eyes with the most memorized verses in the Book: Psalm 23. I believe God is good, but often times the worry in my life would say the opposite: that I don't believe that. Psalm 23 tells us that Jesus is a Good Shepherd. Not a jerk one. Not a manipulative one. Not a tricky one. Not a mean one. God is a Good Father. Not a jerk one. Not a manipulative one. Not a tricky one. Not a mean one.

I don't have to plead for God's goodness. I don't have to earn His love. I don't have to perform at His whim. He doesn't plot the demise of my spirit for His purposes to rule the world while squashing me.

As one of His, through Jesus, He doesn't look at me with condemnation. He looks at me with compassion. He doesn't lead me to slaughter just so he can control me and then tend my wounds so I will love Him. The slaughter has already happened: in the garden and on the Cross. My wounds are already inflicted from my own sin. He tends to them out of His love and mercy, not conspiracy or political agenda. He is love. And I want to reciprocate and share His love.

The Good Shepherd gives us our fill, not always our whims. He leads us to lie down in green pastures beside still waters. He restores the brokenness of our soul and leads us down paths of righteousness for His name's sake, so others may know Him. He doesn't snap and make a barren pasture green for us so we will feel better about the pasture we are in. He leads us through the valleys we have gotten ourselves into or others have put us in, so that we heal, grow in faith, and trust and peace, have no other gods before Him. His plan is for us to live our purpose in true green pastures, true still waters that stay still even when stirred up.

Don't be deceived. Live in the reality of hope and peace not in a manipulation of your perception of reality. He is Living Water – water that can't be bought or earned; it can only be accepted as a gift from the One who leads us to it. But we have to follow. We do need to make our choice. The True Him, not the one we conjured in our minds, but the Him we once knew, for those of us who "used to be Christian" or "used to go to church."

Was it Him that let you down, or did you get deceived or let down by someone else? God doesn't control us like robots.

Whoever pushed you away from Him did that on their own, and He is calling you back. He called me back.

It's important to remember that God is not glorified by our sorrow. He is glorified by our joy. If you left Him, start to turn back. You know where He is. If you don't know Him, have a conversation with someone you know who does. I hope we all have a grandma, an uncle, a neighbor, a friend who has tried to talk about Jesus with us.

Ask your questions; don't just stew in them.

My Grandpa Corky did accept Christ as his Savior several years after the conference. The Lord had put him on many hearts, not just mine, and He answered our prayers one Christmas Eve many years ago. Pa had finally come to the end of his doubts and accepted the gift of salvation through Jesus. He had a changed life even in the few number of years he had left to live it. – *Gracefully Frank*

I was obviously having all the feels over what God was showing me and growing in me. My heart always longs for those friends and loved ones who walked away, or lost faith, or opted out of relationship with Christ like I once did.

Why did we? What were we believing about ourselves or others? Thinking through my wrong beliefs and misunderstandings hopefully gives me an understanding and compassion for them. I pray that my ability to relate with them will open a window for them to relate to a renewed relationship with Jesus.

What's Your Story?

Has God provided support and encouragement to you in surprising or miraculous ways? What made you either believe it was Him, or explain it away as coincidence?

Do you think you have been debilitated in some areas of your life? Has there been death, divorce, fear, or wrong beliefs? Have you asked Jesus to heal you?

Have you ever taken the time to reflect on what developed your current view of God? Who did you listen to? What circumstance set you off on your course of belief? Are those things/people still true or influencing you today? Take a moment to think about how your beliefs about Him developed, and consider if you may need to do a bit of personal investigation.

Return to Regularly Scheduled Programming?

With the pace and surprise of all that was going on, I didn't have time to focus so intently on Land in the way I had been asking for it. I was trying to wrap my head around the Sky that had opened up. Looking back, I can see the shift from demanding my acreage to trying to demand some understanding of His big picture. I went from being so consumed with <u>why</u> God hadn't been doing what I wanted Him to do to constantly wondering <u>what</u> He was going to do next. My shoulders were shrugged, but my heels that had been dug in were starting to have a little lift to them, even though I still assumed India had been the big culmination of all that stretching.

If I had written a thank you note to God it probably would have gone something like this:

Whew, God! We did some things just now! I totally get it! You have ripped off all my little bandages that needed to be ripped off fast or they would hurt worse. Thank you for settling me on back down into what I am comfortable with, and let's put some of the learning to bed. I'm a chicken that you made

courageous. It got a little crazy. I mean Africa and India?!? Whaaaat? But
we made it through. Thanks for fixing me.
Love Always,
Haley.

I set about doing things again in my own understanding. Like Peter going back to fishing (John 21), I went back to work.

I had climbed up my mountains.
I had jumped.
I learned to trust.
I high-fived God.
I went back to normal life and regularly scheduled programming.
And, then, God lit a bush on fire.

In Exodus, chapter 3, Moses was going about his normal routine of tending to his father-in-law's flock on the backside of the desert. Maybe it was just another Tuesday? A regularly scheduled programming kind of day. But, for God, it was the day to call Moses to something greater; and in order to get his attention, God lit a bush on fire.

Anyone been there? In the midst of all the blowing and going, I was a counselor working out what I had learned, feeding His sheep, and getting the hours for my professional counseling licensure. I absolutely loved being in the counseling room with those seeking help and hope and being present to watch God move in their lives. For some, He moved drastically; for others, I didn't get to see Him move – because for whatever reason (maybe them, maybe me, maybe Him), it wasn't time. I was learning and growing and loving the work I was able to be part of each day.

After India, however, it became clear that change was coming: a bush lit on fire, not a real bush, but a clear indication that God would be leading me to do something else, soon. I went through a time of personal attack like I had not experienced before.

In India, God had healed and resolved fears in me by taking me to the very edges of them and giving me the tangible experiences of facing them. In those far reaches, Christ conquered so much fear and doubt, so the enemy had to change tactics.

The new attack was on my credibility and security orchestrated by a person in authority over me. Our battle is not with flesh and blood, even though it is usually flesh and blood that stands before us doing the damage. As the damage intensified, I began to consider relocation options. The details of what and who was going wrong are much less important than the details of what God was doing in the midst of the trial.

I began trying to find my own solutions to separate myself from the circumstance, but what I thought God was using to lead me away from where I was, He was actually using to lead me deeper still to where He wanted me to be. It was another experience when He showed me to be still and know that He is God. I had my eyes open for a way out, but I kept my mouth closed and my feet planted, trusting that God would show me the way.

Seemingly unrelated, I received another e-mail from the international director at our ministry asking if I might consider going to Sri Lanka to help do a training with new partners there. (*This guy has got to be kidding! I am NOT his girl. God and I already did all the things I needed to do in India. I'm all set here. No longer afraid.*) But, somehow, the words that fell out of my mouth were, "Okay, if my boss says I can, I will." The bush that was burning lit the way for me to yes.

It seems as if God's plans for me weren't just to fix me. He wasn't doing all of this refining for my own personal self-actualization and freedom. His plans were for me to fulfill His purposes through me. It was, is, and will always be about Him. I would be packing my bags again for Him, not for me this time.

Yes, His love and freedom are personal to us. He knows us by name and from the time before we were in our mother's womb (Jeremiah 1:5). But when He does all of this in us, we are to be fountains of His life, and not just bottle it up for ourselves. If all this effort were just for my own best life now, what a waste of all this effort. He changed me because there is work to be done.

What's Your Story?

Have you ever thought, "I finally get it? I finally understand everything God is doing and everything I need to do!" How is the lesson that you thought you were learning different than the one you actually learned in hindsight?

Has the enemy ever shifted tactics on you? Are you looking for God in the midst of it? How has God worked it for your good?

First (Wobbly) Leg

Somewhere between India and Sri Lanka, my back got a little stronger, my step a little more sure, and my face a little less worried looking. I had won a battle or two. I had new history to look back on and fresh victories from which to draw strength. I wonder if it was anything like how David felt going into the next battle after the one when he slayed Goliath? Please don't think that I'm doing a battle-to-battle comparison with David, but please do think that I am doing a his-God-is-my-God comparison.

The size of the battle doesn't matter.
The strength of the fighter doesn't matter.
It's God that matters.

God is for us exactly who He was for David. He is the same then, now, and forever. Even though we win some battles, it doesn't mean that it is always smooth flying ...

First Leg – May 15, 2013

Now that I'm all settled in my window seat, and we have reached our cruising altitude, I'm going to back up and write about this day. It's been a good one.

Like clockwork, I woke up 10 minutes before my alarm went off this morning. It seems like every day is busy, but today is one of those days my busy looks a lot different than normal … again. Before my trip to India, I was packed a week early. I was a little nervous leading up to that adventure. Last night, I started putting it all in the suitcase at about 8:30. The Lord has fought and won that battle for me. I'm not who I was.

I got up this morning, walked into the kitchen and slid a Tully's Italian Roast Extra Bold K-cup into my single cup coffee maker and pushed the brew button. Tully's Italian Roast Extra Bold is my favorite coffee when I don't French press Café Bustello in the morning. Have I mentioned I really, really like a good cup of coffee? With my cup full, I sat still with the Lord, Moses, and Jethro in Exodus where Jethro threw a little wisdom down and helped Moses with some strain he was experiencing. Then I spent a little time thanking God for so much I can't express and talking with Him about some other things like this trip, this day, where He is leading, how He is getting me there, and praying for some people I love.

I went for my walk around the park listening to the music that strengthens my bones and courage. Today, I walked to David Crowder Band's, "For A Thousand Tongues To Sing" on repeat. It made my walk a bit more of a march. I have emotionally adopted two doves that I think live in an iris patch in the park. I see them there most mornings. Her name is Harriet. I don't know what his name is. They walk through the irises every morning. The old me would have not thought it was possible to go for a walk before going to the airport. My anxiousness would have kept me home, white-knuckled, praying for safety. I am not who I was though, and I enjoyed my walk.

I arrived at DFW and met up with three friendly faces I work with, with whom I was able to share this journey. All four of us have totally different histories, but for this time, our paths all line up. It is nice to … (pause for turbulence that makes me less able to breathe. Ok, we're lifting up out of the clouds now, and it is starting to get a little smoother … blue Sky back in view).

I've been watching "Pete's Dragon" on the in-flight Disney favorite's channel. I haven't seen this in years. My brother and I used to watch it. In my mind, we watched it a lot, but it may have only been a couple of times, but I know we watched it together. Little sisters remember stuff like that. The dragon always reminded me of my Uncle Cecil. (More bumpy flight. I'm going to try to just keep writing to ignore it.)

When I am afraid, I go to God's Word. Here is my favorite go-to verse for fear: "Fear not, for I am with you; be not dismayed, for I am your God; I will strengthen you, I will help you, I will uphold you with my righteous right hand." (Isaiah 41:10, ESV) I like to think of His righteous right hand under the belly of the plane, and He is flying it around maybe making "zoom" noises. Don't judge. It gets me where I'm going. I'm having to call on this imagery right now.

Back to Uncle Cecil (as I try to not focus on being really high in the Sky and going through some really bad turbulence) … Uncle Cecil was always smiling, and he didn't have teeth, just like Pete's Dragon. That is the kind of thing that sticks out to a little kid. Ugh, this is a bumpy flight, which is why I'm rambling as I write this. I'm trying to focus on something and not freak out. Did you see the movie, Goonies? I kind of feel like Chunk did when the Fertelli's were going to put his hand in the blender. He just started telling stories. I'm just typing away as this plane gets knocked around, reminding myself to breathe; I just realized the bumps have stopped. The clock says 12 hours and 39 more minutes to Dubai. I hope that is the last of it, or you may get to read more about doves at that park (the part where some turbulence began), Goonies, and Uncle Cecil. He would be worth reading about, but that's not my story to tell.

Turns out, that wasn't the last of the turbulence. First of all, there was a bump in the dinner plan as they ran out of saffron chicken before they got to our aisle. The other options were some kind of kidney bean veggie dish (public service announcement: don't eat beans on a plane), or the lamb. I had lamb. I think for the first time ever.

After Anne, Yasmin, and I, the women of row 34 seats A, B, and C (I'm in the window seat) finished eating our meals and visiting a little, I decided to listen to music for a while. I listened to one song and then the turbulence got really bad somewhere high above

Canada. Pull it together, Canada! What we felt before did not even compare. It was probably the worst turbulence I've ever been in, and Yasmin and Anne agreed. I couldn't even write to distract myself because I had death grips on my armrests, and I cried just a little bit.

As the rocky wind beat our plane around until I was nearly sick, the song on my playlist still filling my ears changed, and I heard these words, "Walking stumbling, on these shadow feet ..." Okay, I like this song. Focus on the words. But, then I heard these words, "When the world is falling out from under me ..." STOP LISTENING TO THESE WORDS! Panic. *Lord! I don't want the world to fall out from under me!!!* I quickly yanked my phone up to change the song, but, before I could hit forward, I heard the next words, "I'll be found in You, still standing ..."

Okay, Haley. Be still. I'm going to ride out this turbulence, and I'm not going to change this song. Figuratively, the world has fallen out from under me before. Now I'm in a literal position of the world falling out from under me, but, "I'll be found in You, still standing."

I'm not who I was. He has made me new. He makes me new. Sometimes I don't enjoy it. Sometimes my gut drops out from under me, but He is faithful regardless of the smoothness of the ride. I kept reminding Him that He calms the sea with just a word, and I begged Him to speak calm into the wind. Then He reminded me that while the disciples on the boat were panicking during the storm that had the wind all kicked up, He was sleeping because there was no need to panic (Mark 4:35-41). It's the same in the Sky as in the waves.

The seatbelt light is finally off. I'm going to try to nap and breathe deep again. I did have an opportunity to share Isaiah 41:10, the verse opened up in my Bible on my lap, with Anne and Yasmin after that was all over. So, I would go through that again, but, I really don't want to.

I was able to get some uncomfortable sleep. It's kind of like spending 15 hours in a 4'x1' box. If those calculations aren't reasonable, whatever. It's a small space. I didn't get to watch all the movies I planned on watching. Timothy Keller is to blame. I'm reading, *The Meaning of Marriage.* Don't get hung up in the irony. Being single, I hard-rolled my eyes when a friend, Carissa, suggested it, but I agreed to give it a read anyway. It is a great book that I will start suggesting and buying for friends and family. Married or not. It's so good. Read it. Read anything Tim Keller writes.

When I woke up, I looked at the onboard map of where we were. Flying over Bagdad. That's where we were. Out of scud missile range, though, I'm sure. I saw an oil rig burning in the middle of the Gulf and several ships that I imagined were filled with pirates. We are now entering our final descent into 99 degree Dubai. We'll have an 11-hour layover and have received hotel vouchers. I'll go to a room now and relax and stretch. – *Gracefully Frank*

What's Your Story?

What Bible verses come to your mind in times of stress, fear, or even joy? If you don't have one that comes to mind, consider doing an internet search such as "Bible verses about fear" and find a verse you can lean on.

Have you ever conquered something in your life but find yourself tempted by it still? My fear is conquered (I no longer live by it), but I am still tempted with it at times. If you can relate, what do you do to stay strong?

Sky

I think right about here is where I began to take root in the Sky. The expectation of Land as I recognized and longed for began to be replaced by the anticipation of knowing God in bigger, less sensible ways than I had ever considered. What is God like outside of Baptist, Oklahoma, marriage, and motherhood? I know He is good in those things, I'm so grateful for those things. Those are the roots God gave me ... but those things are not everywhere. My view of Him was expanding, and it needed to expand.

He began showing me His consistent presence and His consistent faithfulness – way outside my box. I understood so much more, yet infinitely less than I thought I did before. For many, He chooses to show Himself through their Land, their spouse, their children. But, for some reason, He has given me the Sky to view Him through. All I can do is tell you about Him from here.

Supplies – May 22, 2013

After my last post, I joined my co-workers for a late dinner in the hotel before heading to the airport at midnight Dubai time. Time becomes kind of a non-factor after a while, and the Dubai Airport is kind of amazing. Both understatements. There were military guards throughout the airport wearing sage green uniforms, all with bodies built exactly the same, as if genetically modified, and wearing red patent leather boots. I really wanted to take a picture of them, but also I really didn't want to get arrested. The ceilings and columns and lights and fountains are beautiful. They put on a good show. We met three college grads from Texas in the customs line. They were headed to Thailand for a graduation trip. Brave kids. I was hoping to get a little sleep on that five-hour flight from Dubai to Colombo, Sri Lanka, and I ended up sleeping the whole time. Except for about a 15-minute window where I opened my eyes and realized the sun was about to rise. Watching the sunrise from an airplane is awesome.

Then we landed in Sri Lanka. Their airport looks a little different than Dubai's airport. It reminded me a lot of the Addis Ababa airport. I think I feel about Addis the same way we think of our first love fondly our whole lives. (Unless your first love was a jerk, then it's not a good comparison.) Going to Ethiopia with Jess was the first time I knew for sure God was calling me to go, and what He did through that trip has strengthened me for each journey since.

We checked into our hotel and had a few hours to rest before having lunch with the Sri Lankans who were joining our training and who quickly became our friends. Thursday night, we had a time of worship together and introductions. All day Friday and Saturday we conducted the conference sessions. Saturday afternoon, the majority of us took an excursion into Colombo before having one final session and dinner on the beach together.

The hotel had a DJ set up on the beach as their Saturday night entertainment, and he played songs from the "Dirty Dancing" soundtrack and what must have been Billy Ocean's greatest hits album. Surreal moment #432: *Am I really having dinner on a beach in Sri Lanka listening to* Hungry Eyes?

On Sunday, one of my co-workers got on a plane to India to do another few days of trainings. The three of us who remained went to a church service with some new friends, toured the orphanage they are building, the daycare they are running, and then went to the site of the newest Hope Center they are opening in the slums of Colombo. I am not sure they ever sleep.

In counseling, and especially in the ministry I work for, we talk a lot about getting to the heart of the matter. Here is the heart of the matter of this trip for me: "And my God will supply every need of yours according to His riches in glory in Christ Jesus." (Philippians 4:19, ESV) I remember thinking of this after leaving Ethiopia, how in a place where irrigation systems aren't available, God sends the rain every day to water their crops. He meets their needs.

In Sri Lanka, king coconuts are everywhere. They are like big hollow coconuts filled with sterilized water for drinking. Literally, the water grows on trees. Many in this part of the world choose to worship manmade idols that offer no hope, only rules. Yet the God who created them still supplies their needs by the fruit of the tree. His eye is on the sparrow, even while allowing them the consequences of their choices. While He waits for them to be told of His grace, He sends them water. – *Gracefully Frank*

I'm still not over those yellow king coconuts. If you sometimes wonder what God is doing, this is just one tiny example. He is being merciful, gracious, and patient. "The Lord is not slow in keeping His promise, as some understand slowness. Instead He is patient with you, not wanting anyone to perish, but everyone to come to repentance." (2 Peter 3:9, NIV)

What's Your Story?

Has there been a time in your life when you were not seeking or following God, but in hindsight, you can see that He continued to provide for you and protect you? What did He provide you? How did He protect you?

Pray for eyes to see how God has given you your own version of king coconuts, and spend some time thanking Him.

Once Upon a Time

Just a few months after that last once-in-a-lifetime trip to Sri Lanka, I was packing my bags to go again. It turned out that none of these trips were to be once-in-a-lifetime but the beginnings of my own story with the Lord. My heart was kind of bursting with all of the things God was doing, and my head could not really understand it all.

His faithfulness was unfolding before me.
His plans,
His path,
His purpose.

He had work for me to do, Land for me to claim, and Sky for me to sail through. He is real, and I get to testify to His presence in a story He is writing. His kingdom and my place in it. He was doing everything He promised. Once again, I sat down to write about it and think through how His story was weaving together mine . . .

Once Upon A Time – September 03, 2013

Once upon a time there was a little girl who never dreamed of going anywhere. She liked where she was. She didn't like everything about where she was, but she certainly didn't want to be anywhere else. She had grown up believing in the King who had come to save her (John 3:16), and she tried her best to honor Him, as little she knew of Him.

But then one day, as she was right in the middle of denying Him, He called to her by name and spoke tenderly to her. He knew her. She began to see Him with her own eyes, and see Him for who he really was (Mark 14:66-72, Hosea 2:14-17). She had believed He was the King. She had been obedient to Him because of that, but now she began to fall in love with Him. So, when He asked her to come away with Him, she went (Mark 6:31). While there, He showed her that He was actually the King of Everywhere, not just of where she was born (1 Corinthians 10:26).

She thought she had known that all along, but she realized she wasn't really going the way she should go, if that is what she truly believed (Proverbs 22:6). He showed her that there was nowhere she could ever go where He wasn't there, waiting on her (Deuteronomy 31:6). He told her that He had loved her and had taken care of her all along because He had plans for her (Jeremiah 29:11). He became her shelter and protector (Psalm 18:2). Sometimes He led her through a wilderness to humble and test her and provided her manna when there was nothing else (Deuteronomy 8:16). He would send her rain when she prayed for it (James 5:18). He would make His face to shine upon her (Numbers 6:24-26). He counted her tears and comforted her when news of loved ones from home made her cry (Psalm 56:8).

He strengthened her, dealt bountifully with her, and gave her rest (Isaiah 41:10, Psalm 116:7). When she lifted her eyes to the hills, she could always see Him there (Psalm 121:1-2). In the morning, He reminded her that He loved her and told her the way she should go because she trusted Him (Psalm 143:8). Where He went, she went. His people were her people (Ruth 1:16). If she had been longing to return to the Land from which she had come, she could have gone. She stayed with Him in the new Land, and He was proud of her (Hebrews 11:15-16).

When she told Him her foot was slipping, He supported her, and when her anxiety was great, He consoled her and gave her joy (Psalm 94:18-19). When she put her hope in Him, He taught her the paths she should take, and her heart was not sick (Psalm 25:4-5, Proverbs 13:12). When there were giants, He gave her stones to sling (1 Samuel 17:40). When there were words to be said, He placed them on her tongue (Jeremiah 1:9). When there were journeys to take, He lit her path by day and by night (Exodus 13:21). He did all of this because she was weak, but He was strong (2 Samuel 22:33). He saved her, quieted her, and sang over her (Zephaniah 3:17). He gave her a new heart and courage (Ezekiel 36:26, Joshua 1:7). Then He led her on a new path, lighting the way as He smoothed the road ahead of her (Isaiah 42:16).

That is what God does.

Through God's Word, we come to know His character. Each of the verses used through this story are written on little cards on my desk. I've leaned on them to remind me of who God is when all I can feel is who I am not. The Bible tells the literal stories of Israel and Jesus Christ to teach us who God is and who we are. He wants us to know Him. He wants us to trust Him when He tells us He has a plan for us and to go where He sends us.

Next week, I'll be back to Sri Lanka because last month I accepted a new position in our international department. Guess what that means? A big part will be travel. If you have read this blog, you know that is not my strong suit. My job now is to daily accept that His grace is sufficient for me, for His power is made perfect in my weakness. My task is to daily call out to Him and to have to trust Him beyond my own perceived strengths.

What an uncomfortable
and perfect gift.

What are you the worst at, Haley?
"Fear."
Well, let's do that, then. My love will cast it out. And I'm going to prove Myself to you and through you. You can say no. You can always say no and run your own show. You did it that way for a long time. I'll bless you, because I am faithful. You'll have some of what you want, all of what you

●   ●   ●

"What are you the worst at, Haley? Fear? Well, let's do that, then. My love will cast it out."

●   ●   ●

131

need, and some of what I'll allow to shape you into who I created you to be. But, as Creator of all the heavens and the earth, My plans for you will be better, and you may begin to walk in them today. I heard you cry out for me. I'm here. I've always been here. I know it doesn't look like you thought. I know your concerns, Haley. I know everything. So, is it a yes, or a no?

"It's a yes."

Okay, then. I will equip you. I am making you new. You are not who you were, so quit telling yourself you are.

This is a condensed representation, not re-creation, of an ongoing conversation in my faith walk with God. P.S. It's never too late to start today.

Since the beginning of the year, I have felt confident that things were changing. I believed and shared with friends that I felt by this fall I would have some clarity on a new direction. I've had a few thoughts on what those changes might be (I always do, and thanks to those who listened to me dream and pursue and wonder). I've taken some steps, done what I believe God has shown me to do in regards to those things, and trusted Him with all outcomes.

Love unconditionally.

Reach out when He shows me.

Say yes when He prompts me.

Go where He sends me.

Stay flexible, hopeful, and sure in Him only.

Months ago, I noticed I was consistently catching the time "8:16," either a.m. or p.m. on my phone, microwave clock, clocks at work, and just on signs and license plates everywhere. At first, I thought I was just realizing that I noticed it more because Mom and Dad's address in Ponca City is 816, and they had just put their house on the market. I thought that was why those numbers were registering to me.

But it kept going, to the point that it was getting comical. I was seeing 8:16 constantly. I looked up all the books in the Bible that have a chapter 8, verse 16, and one pierced my heart: Deuteronomy 8:16, ESV, "(He) who fed you in the wilderness with manna that your fathers did not know, that He might humble you and test you, to do you good in the end."

I can't really explain all the ways that verse is a direct hit for me. Manna has been a big part of my life, taking on many forms since going back to school. "Humbling and testing" ... let me count the ways (even today). But, the line "to do you good in the end," that was a promise God gave me before I left Tulsa one particularly difficult day as I was grappling with the plans He was showing me to leave there and go to seminary. He does me good daily, but I knew when I left Tulsa and when I read this verse again for the first time earlier this summer, that God was up to something specific.

I shared this 8:16 business with a few friends and a few of my family members earlier this summer, and we have laughed about what it might mean beyond knowing God was encouraging me with Deuteronomy 8:16.

A few months ago I was approached about a new job in my current ministry. I was so surprised at the option of it, but honestly I wasn't really sure. The job offer was to go full-time with our International Department. I had known in my heart for months that change was coming, but was this the answer? Taking this job would lock me into Texas and away from completing my counseling licensure. I really thought maybe God was moving me out of here. And, would He move me away from what I thought the point of going to seminary was to begin with?

But, as July drew to a close, I began to know for certain that God was calling me to this plan in particular through others, through His Word, and through the Holy Spirit's confirmation. I prayed God would make it so clear because I wasn't sure my heart was in it, and I needed "courage and clarity" again.

The time frame of being able to officially offer me the job was unknown. I went from hearing, "maybe, January," to, "things seem to be moving fast." I was in no hurry to know one way or the other; I just prayed.

After a couple of weeks of silence, on a Thursday, I received a meeting request e-mail asking if I could meet with my new boss, Phil Prather, and our HR director the next day. That next day was Friday, 8-16-13. They offered me this new position with no idea of the significance of the date. But, I did. I hadn't specifically asked for a fleece moment from God, but He was so gracious and responded to me so personally. He was asking me to do what seemed impossible to me; and, in a very improbable way, He had been preparing me to be confident in it for months.

This is His plan, and I am learning to trust that His plans are better than mine. His timing is better than mine. He will do what He says He will do, and all we have to do is say "yes."

Have you truly sought Him for His plans for you? His plans for you in the next conversation you will have, the next decision you will make, the next prayer you will utter? He loves you. He's been there all along, and when you call on Him, He will come running.

It may not look like you asked, or it may look exactly like you asked. His plans for all of us are tailored to us. My story won't be yours. But, God's character and faithfulness to you will be the same.

– *Gracefully Frank*

What's Your Story?

What is your "once upon a time" story with God? Have you turned to Him to let your story begin?

How has God been personal to you?

Part 3: Liftoff

Where the Trees Talk

2014 was the beginning of three very intense years of going where I never thought I would go. I started trusting deeper than I ever thought I could trust. I became more intently who I was created to be. It became obvious that none of this happened in my own strength, especially to anyone who had been within earshot of my previous anger, complaining, whining, or crying.

At first, I wanted what I wanted: Land. And I wanted it in all the glorious ways I had imagined it. Then I wanted to know God's plan, so I knew for sure I wasn't being a fool in following Him, trusting Him, or doing all these crazy things He wanted me to do. Why couldn't I just be normal? And like everyone else? Somewhere along the path, I finally relinquished the steering wheel. I finally threw the map out the window and began to just go.

All those miles of following Him down paved and dirt roads did not lead me to a homestead; instead they led me to a runway. Actually, to many runways … starting with a runway in Istanbul.

Where the Trees Talk — February 12, 2014

I'm sitting in the Frankfurt airport. I just had some strong coffee, strong potato salad, and a bit of frankfurter. "When in Germany ..." I'm with two co-workers who are just as pleased when we are all together as when we all take a little time to ourselves. I like that in people. I've been walking around the airport shops. Everything is priced in Euros here and expensive. I bought a magnet that looks like a cuckoo clock and has the name "Frankfurt" written on it just below a little man herding goats. It's classy.

When we landed here a little while ago, we walked down those bleacher-looking steps like Jessica and I had in Ethiopia, so I did walk on German asphalt. We didn't make it to soil, which is usually my prerequisite to saying I've been somewhere: I have to actually walk on the Land to be able to claim it. But, I ate potato salad and a frankfurter. I think it counts enough to say I was here and add a magnet to my fridge.

No one here knows it, but in my head I've been going by my alias while walking around. I'm also wearing my new black trench coat. My other coat is red, and according to my boss, it stands out too easily in a crowd. "Someone could track me." So, at Burlington Coat Factory, I got a clearance sale black coat that has some zippers and a turned up collar ... just the kind my alter ego would wear through the airport in Frankfurt; so, she did.

Some of my closest friends know her by name. She's pretty private. She knows Krav Maga, is fluent in every language, even though each language she speaks sounds like high school Spanglish, and her nails are always polished. She shows up when I'm on vacation, feeling a little sassy, pretending to be working undercover, or needing to be brave. I've always had a pretty active imagination, and she is part of it. Judge if you need to.

A couple of Yanks are sitting next to me on their way to Aberdeen, according to the conversation bits I'm overhearing on purpose. They look kind of military. If things go bad here at the airport, my newly devised plan is to jump in whatever vehicle they commandeer and ride things out to the border. I don't even know what border that would be, but I probably won't really need to (it's just for pretend).

I slept most of the flight from Dallas to here, which was great. It was the evening hours at home, but it was the overnight hours where we are headed, so being able to sleep will hopefully work to my advantage. I'm still exhausted after having a bout with the flu last week. There was a woman behind me who kicked my seat constantly. I turned and gave her my best stern look of disapproval in the nicest way possible. Other than the moments she jarred me awake, I slept. I didn't even watch a full movie because we arrived almost an hour ahead of schedule.

Fast-forward a couple of days … it's midnight-thirty, and I'm wide awake. I slept a few hours, but now, after laying here for a while, I'm going to take a minute to write a little, and hopefully tire myself and my brain out.

Istanbul is fascinating. The flight in was probably one of the most amazing sights my eyes have ever seen. It was kind of foggy from a distance, and at first, all I could see were the tallest buildings rising out of the fog, with the ocean water reflected behind them and some mountains. My first thought was, "That looks like a kingdom ... like a Land far-far away, where the trees talk."

We have done one very full day of training and stretching. I love these people. Quickly, I loved them. It seems to usually happen that way. And, it usually seems to happen that our commonalities far outweigh our differences. There is nothing new under the sun when it comes to the heart of mankind and his need for hope. The enemy deceives in the same way he always has, no matter in which kingdom we find ourselves standing. Our weapons to fight him still prove true for freedom when we pick them up, practice using them, increase in proficiency, and take them to battle (Ephesians 6:14-20).

I may not always work in the same place, but I will always do this job. Whether it is working it through in my own life, talking it through with family, friends, community, or in kingdoms that take a long time to travel to or through ... I love it. This is totally the opposite of who I was, but still who I've always been – just redeemed and made new for what He has called me to. There is no explanation for where I sit other than God IS. With Him, even when we are seemingly defeated, victory awaits! (That last sentence is best read in a Scottish accent, just to improve the quality of your reading experience.)

I had my first shawarma sandwich today and, to my friends' embarrassment, I asked for ketchup. After dinner at a local restaurant, I asked to be pointed to the restroom. A non-English speaking waiter took me through two sets of doors and up a few steps that seemed uncomfortably far from my friends. We walked into a large room that was obviously a Turkish nightclub. Thankfully, it was not too late in the evening so I didn't have to fight off invitations to dance.

To my left was a glassed-in office with more than likely a Turkish mob boss and either his right- or left-hand man (okay, more imagining) in a heated and cigarette-smoky conversation (that part not imagined). I smiled and said hi, forgetting to remind myself not to, as I quick marched to the "WC" (water closet) directly ahead. I stepped into the bathroom, saw the stalls and then thought, *That's weird to have a urinal in the women's restroom.* As the reality of where I stood dawned on me, I turned around and walked out of the men's restroom and over to the ladies' room. My angels stay busy. It's not all kingdoms and trench coats. You can take the girl out of Oklahoma, but ... I think I can maybe put a period there and get some sleep now.

Tonight is a new night. Not sleeping last night made today kind of difficult to get through, but thankfully it was still really great. It was our second full day of training, and we've got one more with this group tomorrow before we meet with another partner, then fly to our next destination. This being my personal blog, I stay mostly to my own perspective and story of the events that happen. This isn't the time or place to share their stories. I don't want to take liberties, and I definitely want to be respectful of their trust and privacy. There are times it is okay to share, and times it is better not to share. That is why you don't read a lot about the other people I'm with or the specific events that are happening, but you do get some king coconuts and mob bosses. Things are going great, conversations are fruitful, and good things are happening. Thank you to everyone who is praying for us. — *Gracefully Frank*

Flying into the kingdom.

My alias and my coat having lunch.

Faces and places
that we passed by
on our journey.

The view overlooking a kingdom from a castle.

Trees that talk.

What's Your Story?

Have you ever been on a difficult journey that you were unsure of where you were going? Where did it lead you, and what did you learn?

Have you allowed God to take over your path and lead you to His destination for you? If you have never sought Him for His will for your life, why?

Is there a time you can recall that God protected you when you walked in a wrong direction?

Believing is Seeing

You read that correctly. We are more used to hearing those words in the opposite order: "seeing is believing." That order may work for a marketing campaign trying to get us to buy something, but with God, seeing most often comes <u>after</u> believing. After the step of faith, after we believe, we see the reality of what is …

Believing is Seeing – March 25, 2014

Maybe not all, but probably a lot of us remind ourselves through our daily thoughts and choices of who we used to be. We are reminded by others and by the enemy of the old things that, according to His Word, passed away when we accepted Christ as our Savior and Lord. They are not now. They are no more. They have not been for a while because Christ has cleared them away and set us free. But, we remember and we're reminded. Some days we try, and some days we are successful, to breathe life into old habits. We relive old hurts even though they are behind us. Then we can feel guilty and afraid. We didn't and can't forget, so they must still be here.

I am afraid.
I am prideful.
I am addicted.

The old things are what we know, what we learned to expect of ourselves. They are what we think people still see and what we are afraid we will still find. This is a perfect example of when to apply God's Word. If our belief of who we are is in contradiction to what His Word is saying about us, then we are believing a lie.

It's easy to believe the lie because we have our history or proof to back it up. The truth of who God is transforming us to be is a hope we can't yet see; until we believe and begin to walk it out, we won't see it. If we are looking back, we can't see ahead.

"Therefore, if any man is in Christ, he is a new creature, the old things passed away; behold, new things have come."
(2 Corinthians 5:17, NASB)

"Behold, new things have come ..."

I have to remind myself of this often. I'm really good at reminding myself of all of my insecurities, inabilities, insufficiencies, anxieties, and fears. I can remind myself easily of the failures.

Relationship failures.

Achievement failures.

Grace failures.

So when I come up to new relationships, new tasks or journeys, new grace to give or receive, my first thoughts many times are to rehearse the ways things haven't worked before ... those insecure conclusions I've drawn from those failures. Those are the rocks I have found myself trying to stand on at times.

Confident in discouragement because I believe I already know how something will end based on the old things.

Old fears, old insecurities, and the times I wasn't enough.

Not strong enough,

smart enough,

pretty enough,

good enough,

classy enough,

close enough,

far enough,

young enough,

old enough.

Sometimes instead of not enough, I've been too much.

Too independent.

Too loud.

Too strong. (It turns out that I have needed to be strong.)

We operate under the "seeing is believing" mindset. I haven't seen me new, so I don't quite believe it yet. But faith is believing in things unseen (Hebrews 11:1). What we believe determines how we operate. God keeps reminding me through His Word and His Spirit to do things differently than I've always done them; and I remind Him of how it's always been, justifying my insecurity. *You are not who you were, I am making you new,* He says. But I remind him, *Look at my proof of who I am.* Then, in His great patience, He reminds me to *look at the proof of who I AM. Now, maybe have a seat (on an airplane) and hush a little bit, Haley.*

In Christ, either the old things passed away, or they didn't.

Either His Word is true or it isn't.

Either I believe it or I don't.

I'm convinced it's true 100 times over, so the problem lies in my belief, not in His truth. Though the Father of Lies deceived, distracted, and tried to destroy my life for years, I'm coming to the belief, finally, that through Christ I've been enough all along. I'm realizing that all along I was allowing people and circumstances to determine otherwise. I let them have the authority that only He has over me.

I am enough, not because of me but because He is my strength, and I can do all things through Him. His grace is sufficient; I cast my anxieties on Him, and I will fear no evil. The new things have come. They are now. They are for always and ever. His Word, applied to my life, changes my life in all the good ways.

I'm learning not only that I'm enough but that those I love are enough too. They don't need to be conformed to my image for them. God already has a plan for them. Free to be loved and free to love. Free to go and to stay. Free to try and sometimes to fail. Transformed by the renewal of the mind.

Some of you may not have any insecurities, or you may have resolved all this with God at a much earlier time in life than me. We all have different journeys, and humbly I'm laying mine out for you now. It's part of the trusting Him and obeying His prompting to share my story that points back to Him (just in case someone reading this can identify).

What is new about you since Christ took over? Take a little inventory to give thanks and remind yourself of who He is and who you are in Him. What do you keep reminding Him, or yourself, about who you were? That is where you need to be reminded that "the old things have passed away; behold, new things have come." *Believe and see.*

Every time the Lord takes me to share His hope with others, I get to live again the radical *new* that has come since Christ. I was slow to give Him the reigns, and I have a lot of old things to remember.

My flesh tries to remind me to be afraid to feel insecure and I still get attacked, but my Savior reminds me I'm enough, I am new, already and forever. He reminds me through His Word and through His Spirit, *I am your Savior and your Lord now, and I am doing a new thing. I know the plans I have for you. I love you with an everlasting love … and have all along. I am not who you've been afraid I was, and you are not who you've been convinced you were. Put the chains down. I am in you. You are new. Believe and see. Go and do. Love and trust.*

That is true for all of us who are in Christ, not just for someone working in ministry, or who went to seminary, or whatever other qualifier you may use to disqualify yourself.

You are loved by God and the Savior of the world. You can choose to deny it, but it doesn't change it. You can choose to not accept it, but that doesn't mean it isn't there for you. You can stay who you always were, or you can become who you were always meant to be: loved and free, right where you are. "Therefore, if any man is in Christ, he is a new creature; the old things passed away; behold, new things have come." (2 Corinthians 5:17, NASB).

I spent most of the weekend preparing for the next trip that begins this coming Sunday. I will be gone for 23 days, home for eight, then gone again for nine, in Albania, Italy, Sri Lanka, Turkey, Georgia (not the one known for peaches), and Germany.

The more I believe, the more I see. The more God works His grace into my life, the more opportunities He gives me to pour it out into others. Those who know me best, and have seen me at my worst, know that only God could take me from where I was and bring me to where I am and then faithfully to where I'm going. He is as real as you sitting there reading this.

He knows you.

He loves you.

He wants you to know Him.

He is my confidence. His Word, not my past, is the rock and truth I now stand on. Believing is seeing. — *Gracefully Frank*

What's Your Story?

When it comes to trusting and believing God, have you been waiting to "see" something happen first? "I'll believe when _____ happens." Or maybe, "I don't believe because _____ has happened."

Do you have a memory or experience where your faith and conviction to believe allowed you to see God in a new, more personal way? What did you learn about God's presence in your life?

Connecting Dots

What if we could raise high above the story of our life, way up in the Sky, to see how each moment, each event, each friend, and each circumstance played a role in directing our beliefs and our path? We could see the moments on the playground where we were left out, or the moment when we got the part in the play, or the grandparent who prayed for us, or the friend who invited us to church, or the loved one who betrayed us.

What if we could rise up and see God's presence and the moments we said yes or no to Him? What if we could see where He was and what He was working out for us and how it all connected? That would be cool.

That is what living a life of faith can do for us. We can look back in hindsight and see what God was doing – how He was equipping, protecting, or leading us. For instance, David was a patient shepherd who became the king of men. He killed a lion on the roadside, and, eventually, a giant on the battlefield. We can read how each step equipped him for the next to give him faith, courage, and the skills he would need to be the man after God's own heart.

When we look at the lives of those in Scripture, we are basically lifted way up to see their circumstances and God's character, compassion, mercy, sovereignty, and justice in their lives. We can see God's plans for them and believe that God has a plan for us.

The further I have been lifted into the Sky, the more clearly I have been able to see His presence and working throughout my own life. I see how God has been equipping me all along to be prepared to go where He leads me today, beginning all the way back at church camp.

Did God have other plans for me? Would I be living a different life if I had been more obedient from the start? Would those plans look more like the Land I've been wanting? Or, did He allow my wandering, my moment in that cave, my experiences in regret and loss to have me right where He has me today?

With all of my heart, and now with all of my time and experience in surrender to the Lord, I still do not fully know the answer to that. Am I living His Plan A, or B, or maybe even C? Or, was this current life His plan for me all along? I deeply search His Word and promises as I try to understand the life He has given me and not fear or faint when …

I consider the reality of never having children.

My heart is on edge at the thought of never being loved by a spouse.

I find myself on a safari in Africa.

I'm in a car going up a Himalayan mountainside in Nepal.

I'm singing hymns in a 13th century church looking out at the peak of Mt. Ararat.

This dramatically different life than I expected has me clinging to this hope: I believe God had a purpose in creating me and that He has a design and a path for me. Based on His Word, I believe His ultimate purpose is to conform me to the likeness of His Son (Romans 8), and to reconcile me to Himself (2 Corinthians 5) to glorify Him and be a light to others seeking Him (Matthew 5). My free will to choose Him or not choose Him at different times in my past has determined what paths have opened before me. I believe this for you, too.

Maybe there was a Plan A, and maybe that was derailed by my own will and choices. Maybe I blew it and not having the Land I prayed for is my consequence. Maybe everything else will always only be second best or less than what could have been. Maybe you can relate to that feeling. If that were the case, then I would be right to feel hopeless. If I missed my one boat, then I should live in constant regret of the past and the choices I made.

But …

If Plan A was only *one* option of getting me to His ultimate purpose in creating me, if with Christ I cannot miss my life purpose even after having missed a few boats, then whether I am on Plan A or Plan B, I have hope. When I turn to the Lord in repentance and devotion, and leave the plan-making to Him, then His big-picture purpose for me is still on in full force.

No matter my mistakes, age, marital status, Facebook status, weight, wardrobe, job, or hobby, what God has planned for me or through me will be, when I follow Him. I have not missed "it" because "it" lies ahead of me, not behind me. The fulfillment of my life is secure, and I am striving toward it full of hope.

Whether we are on Plan A or all the way to plan Z, even though we may mourn, we do not need to despair over failure during different times in our lives or forever stand on one success.

We could grow in bitterness over a missed plan or Land that we wanted. We could get stuck in heartbreak, mistakes, and failure. Getting stuck is when life gets wasted. Instead, we can realize all those plans – A through Z – have the same end goal that we can begin striving toward today. If you are married, your spouse is part of that plan. If you have children, they are part of that plan. If you don't, he is still working a plan in your life.

All plans have been means to grow and learn and heal and be made new according to His will for us. When we turn to Him, nothing – no missed opportunity, unsuccessful plan, hurt, or heartbreak – can separate us from His ultimate goal for me or for you.

This is how His mercies are truly new every morning.
This is why I do not live in regret.
This is why it is never too late to turn to the Lord.

Whatever plans you have made, succeeded in, or failed to execute, they do not determine your final destination or your joy for the morning. Only your decision about Jesus Christ and your decision to seek and follow the Lord will result in fulfilling your purpose and get you on the right plan. Maybe my Plan A would have included children, and maybe my plan K does. Maybe in Plan A, I would have never left Oklahoma, but the plan I'm on now has taken me to thirty-three countries. I don't think countries take the place of children in God's blessing, but I am thankful and rejoice in what He gives me. I'm letting God write the story now. I write and share what has happened to tell you of His faithfulness.

I know that going back is not an option and going forward is a gift. I believe that the good God has planned for me now does not require redoing or undoing anything in my past. I don't know what might have been, but I know what is now. The Apostle Paul said it this way, "But by the grace of God I am what I

"... the good God has planned for me now does not require redoing or undoing anything in my past."

am, and His grace toward me did not prove vain ..." (1 Corinthians 15:10a, NASB)

Although the desire for Land the way I have traditionally viewed it is still there, my expectations have drastically changed as I lay my life at His feet from my aerial position in the Sky.

There have been moments with people in places I never dreamed of seeing and living – moments I would not have even known to ask for – but moments that now make up the life I'm incredibly grateful to live. His grace toward me is not in vain.

These are the moments, the fulfillments of His promises, that I cherish in my heart because of what God has done.

Moments like these in Sri Lanka ...

Church Youth Camp – April 18, 2014

It's raining again here in Sri Lanka. They are in a severe drought, and this rain sounds furious about it. The thunder and wind are intense. The electricity comes and goes, and the streets outside my window that have been busy with tuk-tuks, buses, and ladies walking with colorful umbrellas to block the sun have emptied. Only the water rushes down the street now. I ordered my afternoon tea just in time. We have an hour until dinner, and then we will join the campers for the final night of the youth camp, to be capped off with a bonfire if the rain stops. That will be surreal moment #473. Standing near a bonfire in Sri Lanka on Good Friday. I never would have imagined this, not in all my days.

Casey, my friend/co-trainer this week, and I have thought about our own experiences at church camp in Oklahoma: Falls Creek. We went back in the days when you couldn't wear shorts and service was in the old outdoor tabernacle. If it was raining, you got wet. If it was hot, you sweat. It's not a lot different here. They have a theme song they have sung in the mornings each day here in Sri Lanka. It reminds me of how we used to have a main theme song throughout the week at Falls Creek. One summer the lyrics for our theme song included, "*Jehovah Jireh, my Provider, His grace is sufficient for me, for me, for me ...*" They have been playing in my head all week. That song has stuck with me for well over 20 years, even though I refuse to accept that it was well over 20 years ago when I first heard it.

Falls Creek ... happy sigh. I'm so thankful for the faces that come to mind that I shared those weeks of life with, those laughs, those tears, those moments of faith and surrender, icees, volleyball, gum tree, and walking around forever ... and the moments my heart about beat out of my chest with love and calling for Jesus Christ. I hope the kids here this week have made as sweet of memories and that the Lord has imprinted on their hearts a love for Him that will not fade. His love for them never will, even if their love does, and He will draw them back to Himself.

He doesn't let us roam far away from Him when we are His. Case in point: I'm unspeakably thankful He came after me. If you have wandered from your first Love, you should know that He is coming for you. He still loves you. It can all be water under the bridge as soon as you are ready. He will wash years and tears and fears down the river. (I know that is a lot of rhyming, but I like word pictures.)

What would Him washing those things away for you look like? What would Him drawing you back into close relationship with Him look like? Or building a relationship with Him for the first time? Grace is a wonderful gift, whether it's the first time you receive it or the eleventy-billionth.

This morning I had the opportunity to lead both morning sessions. It was a sweet time I will not soon forget. I am so thankful for how God provided for our preparation time and for the hearts of these campers who are living the after-effects of a civil war with loving hearts to serve God and ready smiles to greet these two visitors from the U.S. who sweat a lot and don't speak their language. I can't quit waving at them and saying hello, just to see their smiles.

I'm inspired by our partners here who have gotten little to no sleep but never complain. They are so thankful to be able to provide a camp like this for these young people. It has been three years since their last camp. Many of those serving here were at the last camp and now have a changed-life testimony the other young people can witness. Praise the Lord! I am ready to be home, but today I wouldn't want to be anywhere else.

Tomorrow morning we will start back toward Colombo. Our first flight home begins in the earliest hours of morning on Sunday. Easter Sunday. After three flights and about 24 hours travel time, we'll be home. – *Gracefully Frank*

The rain stopped and the bonfire was lit.

What's Your Story?

Do you find yourself longing for a different life, regretting what lies behind you? What was life supposed to look like? What could you do today to begin looking forward instead of backward?

If your story with the Lord were in Scripture, what would the lesson be that the reader would learn?

What ways can you see God connecting dots between your past with Him and your present?

The Unexpected

Have you ever felt like God was really leading you in a direction you didn't want to go, and as soon as you finally said okay, you ended up not having to go there? Is that some kind of trick? "By no means," as Paul would say when trying to gently state the obvious.

> But, it is a testing of our hearts.
> It is a refining of our will,
> the molding of our clay,
> the check of our engine,
> the de-icing of our wings before liftoff.

I could probably go on. The older I get the more I know to say yes fast and early. Not yes to everyone and everything, just yes to Him, every time.

When I finally truly meant it, when my heart was actually lined up with my mouth and my steps, when I had tasted God's idea of honey, seen the fruit of what He was asking me to do, and jumped off the cliffs He led me to, then, He gave me home.

Home was Land I had underappreciated as I tried to replicate it in my own life. My disappointments nearly choked out my blessing of home. But, in taking me away from it, He gave it back to me more fully, more beautifully than I had ever looked at it before. Maybe this is a bit how the Prodigal was feeling as he looked up the road toward his dad running out to him. Home was sweet again.

Home Sweet 'Homa – July 11, 2014

I've begun packing again. Not for a trip, but for a move. The move back to Oklahoma. Happy sigh. It was seven years ago this month that I committed to moving to Texas and beginning that long haul at seminary. And now as these boxes get taped up, I'm committing to move home. It's kind of hard for me to believe, but it is definitely happening.

I have certainly not been shy about how much I love home (definition of home: Oklahoma, where I come from, and the general vicinity where most all my family live – "most" is for my cousin Lane who is here in Texas). Where the waving wheat smells sweet. (Disclaimer: I haven't actually spent a lot of time smelling waving wheat in Oklahoma). Home is where my parents are. Where cancer is present and, even more importantly, where it isn't present. Where my Grandma's voice can still be heard in person. Where my brother, and the four people he brought into our life, live and love and are in plays and ballgames and like to drink coffee on the porch. Where some of my life-long and favorite friends are a couple of miles away instead of a state and a couple of months away (some of my other favorite friends will remain here in Texas.).

Home is where the Lord first called me, second called me, and now for the third time has called me back to serve Him. That is where I am moving. The place where I can live life to serve the Lord, *and* be the daughter, sister, and friend I love to be. Okla*homa*. I know the step toward home isn't always the next one for everyone. I cannot type out words to explain how grateful I am for this to be the next step for me.

I had a friend ask me a while back why I didn't just move there already, if that is where I wanted to be. My decision is to believe in who God is and trust His Word, His plans, and His Spirit to guide me. I trust that when He says He has plans for me – for life, for ministry, for relationships, for purpose – He means it, and that it's concrete, not in theory, not in general to humanity ... but for me (and for you). And I (you) can rely on His timing and trustworthiness to reveal it.

I could have chosen to move home several times over the past couple of years: when Dad got sick, when other family members were hurting beyond what I would consider reasonable. When I experienced difficulties and trials here in Texas, I could have manipulated the truth that God wants what is best for me and declared that would mean God would want me to move home.

I could have dug to justify returning home, but there wasn't peace when I tried to find a loophole to get me back there. Peace only came in the "be still." Had I gone home before, it would have been in my own strength and wisdom.

Like a loving Father, He would not have abandoned me; He doesn't do that. He would have still worked. He would have still shown me, but there probably wouldn't be the joy, like there is now, in knowing it's Him who is making the way instead of me digging one out.

I had decided several times that I would stay and root here in Texas, say yes to everything, dig in, and be present, but again, His ways are higher than mine. A good reminder to not resolve myself to what I think is the plan but to resolve myself daily to the Plan Maker. You don't waste as much time that way.

When I took my current ministry position, I thought that was the final plan: I will be in Texas (I'm always trying to get to that final answer moment). I knew for certain on August 16th that this job was where God was leading. I had no idea that this job, the one I thought was locking me in to Texas, would be the very way God would bring me back to my home Land.

God is good and faithful. He gives the wheat and the honey. Just like He told me He would. Getting to work from home and move to Oklahoma isn't the proof that God is good or faithful. That truth was never contingent on where I live. He just is, and we just have to *Believe* and *See*.

Because of the nature of this work, and the heavy travel involved, my position has been opened to be a remote work position; this allows me the opportunity to be surrendered to the work He has called me to and have time to build into home and family. Now, as I continue to go to Lands He calls me to, w*here the trees talk* and hope is needed, I will get to come home to the people I love. I will continue sharing about discipleship and transformed lives over there and can live that out with the family God has given me here.

I don't know exactly what that will look like, but I know that's what He is doing. My life is transformed through my relationship with Jesus Christ and the power of God's Word. I'm not who I was because of who He is. And I like it. I like to share it.

I like to talk frankly about it.

I like to show others it is possible.

I live to honor Christ and His authority in my life through living out this change. I am getting to serve Him in ways that are incredibly difficult for me … and that I love more than I imagined possible. And now, I get to do that from *home sweet 'homa*. I might burst. I will still cross the Red River southbound often, but I like to drive; I like to sing in the car. I like to stop in Ardmore, Oklahoma, and get a coffee. I have a few deeply sweet friendships here in Texas that I will miss so much, that will make it easy to come back this way.

In a time of devotion with friends this week, we were asked what we think of when we hear the word "surrender." I realized that seven years ago, surrender to me meant: giving in, loss, insecurity (leaving my job and going to school), and fear. But I was committed to it because He had made it so ridiculously clear. Surrender meant obedience. I thought mostly about what I would have to do in that surrender. But, the first words I listed on my paper this week were: release, freedom, new life, and letting go, just like Elsa walking up a snow-covered mountain.

It immediately struck me how different surrender looks now. Now, I think more about what <u>He</u> will do when I surrender. It's not loss anymore; it's life. It's gain. One step at a time. Blind and weak; bold and certain. It's no longer just about obedience. I surrender because now, even when it's hard, my heart wants to be wherever He sends me.

I don't ever want to be anywhere else. I will step on whatever wave He tells me to step on (and there have definitely been some hard waves that have been scary to step on). But, case in point, as I pack up my little one room efficiency apartment here in Plano sometimes those waves are exactly where you want to step, and you kind of do the happy dance as you put your foot down. Guess what I'm doing right now? – *Gracefully Frank*

* * *

I thought mostly about what <u>I</u> would have to do in that surrender ...
Now, I think more about what <u>He</u> will do when I surrender.

* * *

What's Your Story?

Have you ever surrendered something to the Lord, and He gave it back to you?

Have you been tempted to move (to a place or to an action) before you knew the time was right? What happened? What have you learned in hindsight? How will you avoid that in the future?

Do you sometimes struggle waiting on God? Talk about it with Him. Consider writing out a letter to Him so you may express your thoughts clearly. Then listen for His encouragement.

Tonight from Zimbabwe

I have often confessed to people that every time the plane touches down, I'm a little bit surprised. There may be no going back to living fear-based if you're following the Lord, but it doesn't mean the temptation is no longer there. I'm certainly not the flyer of the year.

If I don't get a window seat ...
If they make me check my carry-on ...
If any little semblance of me being in control is jacked with ...

I have to use my super serious tone of voice when I start talking to the Lord about it. I am absolutely not who I was, but I am also absolutely not yet who I will be. It's a process. But, instead of fighting the process, I've learned to lift off with it. Except maybe when elephants try to kill me.

Sweet Grace — September 14, 2014

"The heart of man plans his way, but The Lord establishes his steps."
(Proverbs 16:9, ESV)

One of the best moments of these trips is when I finally buckle into my seat on the first flight out of town. That's the moment I quit planning. If it's not packed, I won't have it. If I don't have a spreadsheet for it, a session plan for it, or an emergency escape plan for it, I will just have to rely on the Lord for it (insert winky face here. I always have to rely on the Lord, sometimes I just forget that). When I buckle in, I truly understand I am at the end of any perceived strength or control I think I have. I just get to go along for the ride, trusting that whatever plans I have made, He will establish my steps.

This is sweet grace to me.

This life the Lord has led me to is not just about the work He is doing through me, but, in His great love, it's also about the work He is doing in me. As my boss says, "Our greatest testimony is our own changed life." I am humbled to dust and so thankful He is changing me. I'm coming to realize this God, who I thought just wanted my obedience, also wants my heart. He wants me to know His love, and then share His love unconditionally with others. No comparisons. No guilt trips. No hidden agendas waiting around the corner. He loves us. He makes a way for us. He establishes our steps if we will just let him. My steps to Oklahoma, my steps to Zimbabwe, and whatever steps He has for me next — all for Him. I like this life. Unscripted, but not unestablished. Not unplanned. Just unknown by me.

I am definitely in one of my happy places when I have the opportunity to share His hope and the truth of His Word. To see understanding in the faces in front of me, to see some well up with tears, to have them afterward tell me what they are getting from God's Word and especially how they realize that they have not understood their identity in Christ, but are so thankful for the teaching from the ministry through which I serve the Lord. They come to know where the work needs to begin: first in themselves and then in those they disciple and counsel.

You guys, I would go all the way to Zimbabwe if I had to, to take this message to people ... oh wait, I'm already here. I didn't write the resources that share God's Word so practically. God gave that assignment to the founder of our ministry. But I am so thankful He has given me the honor to carry it around the world because I am a living testimony of His faithfulness.

We are doing three two-day meetings in Zimbabwe and one two-day meeting in Zambia. Today is a complete day of rest, the first since we arrived that is not a travel or training day. We walked down to a shopping area for lunch and to a craft market where I bought a little painting for $10. I am not feeling completely well (don't ask), so lots of water and probably an early bedtime before meetings begin again in the morning. Something to note: Harare smells like Osage County during burn season. It is wonderful to me.

After we arrived in the capital city of Harare, we drove (four hours with no air conditioner and the windows down) to a smaller town. When we arrived, our hotel did not have our reservations.

They had rooms for us that first night, and then a cancellation for us to stay the second night, but made no promise for the third night. *Soooo, we're in the middle of Africa with no reservation? Okay. I'm calm.* #notcalm

We found an African snake on our porch one morning, and I wasn't very chill about it. It was an African snake! On the porch of our bungalow that has a thatched roof and that I can see the Sky through. That snake certainly could have slithered through there and killed me in my sleep. The yard men, obviously not as upset by this as me, killed the devil snake by throwing bricks at it. Then we had African snake blood on our porch. *Maybe I should find a way home now?*

The meetings went so well. The ladies are wonderful and so excited to have counseling help for their community. The Lord is growing their ministry there. It is fun to witness it and get to join them in the work for even a short time. I loved getting to sing and dance with them. I'm afraid I've got rhythm, and I may start busting it out more often. Or maybe just when I'm in a Land far-far away. I love the music here.

The hotel really did not have a room for us the third night, so Rick, one of the people I'm traveling with, spent a few hours trying to find us other accommodations for our final night there. A lot of places were booked, but there was an animal reserve right outside town that had openings. The catch was their opening was for tents down by a river.

Nope.

"I don't do tents down by rivers in Africa."

"I don't really even do tents, or Africa, either one."

"This is not who I am."

After my wise and gracious friend, Kathy, heard my words and read my face, she gently said, "I'm pretty sure this is who you are now; you are going to have to quit saying this is not who you are because here you are, staying in a tent, down by a river in Africa." *Okay. I wonder who else I am that I've been saying I'm not.* I'm sure the Lord will show me.

The tents were nice. They had little beds, a bathroom and monkeys constantly jumping on and about them. There were a lot of strange animal noises all throughout the night. How do I know that? I was awake for quite a bit of it listening to lions talk and the thud of monkeys landing on our tent as they swung through the trees plotting our demise.

We had been pretty nervous (I say *we* only because it makes me feel better) about where we were going to stay that third night, but it gave us a little overnight adventure we did not plan but were blessed to experience. The next day, before we left to drive to the next town, we took an hour safari drive. It was all fun and games until the elephant tried to kill me.

During the safari, we drove into a little grove of trees where three elephants were hanging out. Two of them moseyed over to our truck and started acting a little riled up. Our driver began trying to calm them down as he opened his truck door to address them. He told us to be still and calm. That's when a third elephant came out of the trees and headed straight for me in the open-air truck we were in. In my mind, the elephant was angry and rampaging. In actuality, he was probably smiling and tiptoeing.

Our driver told me not to panic as the elephant's trunk came into my lap to thoroughly investigate me. *Really? "Don't panic?" This seems like an appropriate time to panic. I mean, if ever there were a time to panic, wouldn't this be one of those?* In my quiet, yet panicked voice, I kept whisper-screaming, "I'm very uncomfortable! I'm very uncomfortable!" Thankfully, I was able to refrain from the language in my scared heart. My Zimbabwean friend began pleading the blood of Jesus over me, as my two American friends, Rick and Kathy, were laughing so hard you would think they had forgotten we were in the wilds of Africa!

Thankfully, the elephant did not snap my neck with the brush of his trunk. He did, however, get trunk juice on me (puke) before he strutted away, literally swinging his tail in prideful accomplishment. So now, I have slept in a tent down by a river in Africa and single-handedly tamed a wild elephant. Right? That's how I am going to remember it. It reminds me of a time I almost got eaten by crocodiles in a mangrove in Mexico. I'm starting to sense a pattern.

The next meeting began the next morning. We were so blessed by the way the Lord calls us and equips us. We left right after the meeting to try to get back to Harare before dark because not only is everyone driving on the wrong side of the road, but there are no lane markings on the very busy highway between where we were and where we were going. Thankfully, we only had about an hour to drive after dark, and we made it safe and sound. Skipping dinner, I went straight to bed because put-a-fork-in-me-I'm-done.

Tomorrow we will meet with our in-country committee before starting the third round of meetings on Tuesday. The temperatures here are beautiful. Flowers are blooming, and, when you don't smell something burning, you can smell gardenia and other flowers in the air. I like it here.

It's always difficult to put into words what my heart is beating out. Especially tired, a little puny, and thousands of miles from home. I just want to always share the goodness, faithfulness, and love of the Lord. It's not about the harrowing account of my taming a wild African elephant single-handedly, but I hope you see the reality that God IS.

I'm not trying to say "follow Jesus and you will go to Africa," but follow Jesus and He will give you new life. He will transform you, set you free, and establish your steps to be who He created you to be: His. Loved. Transformed.

I lived a lot of years being someone I was not made to be. Sharing the story of my own changed life through Jesus down this road filled with challenges and sweet grace is the only way I know to shout this from the only mountain top near me at the moment. I hope it makes you want to seek Him, too. Okay. That's all for tonight from Zimbabwe. — *Gracefully Frank*

At the end of this trip, my friends and I paid $20 each to ride a bus seven hours each way and spend one night to see one of the Seven Wonders of the World: Victoria Falls. God gives good gifts, and on that day, He gave me a waterfall.

What's Your Story?

Have you been telling yourself you are not who God says you are? Who have you been saying you are?

What could you do today, or in the near future, to practice believing and being who God says you are?

Are you surprised at who God is leading you to be?

Rejoicing and Assimilating

With each "yes" and each trip, I learn and see more.

More of God,
more purpose,
more beauty in the Sky,
more joy in the journey,
more peace in my spirit.

Last Week In Colombia – January 18, 2016

We arrived in Bogota well past my bedtime several days ago to temperatures in the 70's, sweet friends, and something in the air that made the space between my eyes swell up and my head throb. After a couple of Benadryl that expired in 2012, I was feeling better and ready for the week.

We had a few days of meetings with our partners from around the country. I'm so honored to meet and work with these new friends. After our first two days of meetings, we had some free time before our flight to the next city for the next meeting. Our friends took us on a Colombian road trip.

I love road trips. In a van filled with nine of us, I was the only non-Spanish speaker. I often find myself in carloads for long road trips where I don't understand the language being spoken. I usually slip an earbud into whatever ear is farthest from my friends and kind of tune out from what I don't understand and tune into music that restores my balance. I don't want someone to have to constantly translate to keep me included in the conversation, and it helps me to climb into my own space for a little bit after so much together time with others. For this road-trip in particular, the Avett Brothers crossed the miles with me.

We finally dismounted the van when we reached the Cathedral de Sal Zipaquira, an underground salt cavern that has been turned into a walk through the stations of the cross of the Via Dolorosa. The grand finale is a cross carved out of salt so high I can't describe it. My first panic attack (in what feels like another life now) was in an underground cavern in Branson, MO (scary place), but this time, there was no panic, no attack. I've been made new.

My alarm went off this morning at 3:45 a.m. I thought I would dread that, but I was in the middle of a weird nightmare, so the alarm going off was welcome. Actually, all three alarms from my phone and my friends' phones went off at the same time. We didn't want to oversleep. A melodic dinging, a buzzer, and the song "10,000 Reasons" brought us out of our short night's sleep. We've got a flight to catch. The eight-hour drive to the next city turns into a 45-minute flight when you lift off the roads that wind around the mountains and into the Sky where it's a straight shot.

We met another group of pastors who flew in from a coastal town, where they have begun a ministry center in partnership with our ministry. Our first stop was a place for people to find hope near an apartment community. I do speak a few words of Spanish ("donde es el baño" being probably the most vital), but I understand only about two words when someone is speaking to me. When meeting our friends here, I pray a lot and become an official picture taker, hugger, and cliché American trying to speak the few high school Spanish words I remember.

Our next plan was to drive straight to our hotel for a bit of rest before our next meeting that evening. Instead, our friends decided we needed to see "The Rock of Guatapé." I thought, *A rock?* But this is a little more than a "big rock."

It was worth the drive. It rises up from the countryside and lake at its base so huge and awkward. It's as if it dropped out of the sky. No landform around it is similar. Ancient cultures worshipped it, and the current culture depends on people like us coming to see it. We took a few selfies, I bought a new magnet for my fridge, and we were off again.

We paid for our excursion with another very late night, as it pushed our meetings back a couple of hours. But, how often would we get to see a rock like that?

Then it was meeting day. I love meeting day. It is when I get to experience God's faithfulness in different ways than on all other days. There are language barriers and cultural barriers, and He breaks through them all.

I pray for His Word,

His leading,

His presence,

His will,

and in ways I cannot always describe, He does all of it.

He leads the conversations in directions of His planning, because it certainly isn't mine. Our differences make us more dependent on God during our time together. We can't speak each other's language, we can't relate to our specific cultural histories or perspectives, so we have to focus on what unites us through His Spirit. We get to experience Him without the clutter of our own expectations. It grows my faith and courage to see Him work through us, in spite of us.

Sometimes there are language barriers even when we all speak English, and cultural barriers even when we live in the same town. "Trust in the Lord with all your heart and do not lean on your own understanding." (Proverbs 3:5, ESV) When we apply this verse and start to see others through God's eyes instead of through our own understanding, we will start crossing some barriers because barriers fall apart in His presence.

Our time together was held in a First Baptist church founded by American missionaries many years ago. I was tired, a little emo, and got overwhelmed thinking about the footsteps we were walking in. I am so thankful for their faith and courage. I wonder what God did in their hearts, how He united them, comforted them, provided for them, entrusted them to be there. I hope they get to see a glimpse of the church their faith built and the fruit of their labor growing so abundantly.

I'm home now. I met my family at church today. We sang "Jesus at the Center of It All" with the people of the Church that I worship with on Sunday. I deeply rejoiced at who He is and let those words sink deeper and deeper into my heart, praying they would flow out more and more through my life. *Jesus at the center of it all.*

Rejoice is a word I'm focused on this year. A woman at our ministry encouraged us to pray for a word, and I did, and this is the one that kept coming at me. I wanted my word to be divergent (having become a fan of the movie, "Divergent"), but it wasn't. Rejoice is a great word. As the Lord has graciously directed and redirected my life, He has helped me see more clearly and be better at thanksgiving (thankfully), but, rejoice is the word I think I need to practice.

Rejoice seems like thankfulness kicked up a notch with gladness and maybe a little appropriate dancing. The Bible discusses rejoicing in trials and suffering for we know the outcome and also rejoicing in gladness and praising for the good the Lord has done.

Come what may, this will be a year of rejoicing. Rejoice. He is truly the center of it all. I'll let you know how it goes.

— *Gracefully Frank.*

Cultural Assimilation – February 10, 2016

Sometimes I practice my Dirty Harry face. I squint up my eyes and kind of squinch up my lips to try to look a little more tough and a little less like a target as I walk through crowded streets in far-away Lands. Our partners are always so attentive and try to protect me/us from people who may be willing to risk taking a chance on me to get my backpack or phone. That kind of thing could happen anywhere, but there have been a few places lately where we had to think about it a little more.

I've been told I do not blend in well, so I do a little extra to look like someone who may not blend in but is not easy to mess with. I'm sure it works. Sometimes I sneak a smile at someone whose eye I catch. Especially if they are very young or very old. Have I mentioned I love older people? What if no one else has been friendly to them today? What if they prayed for someone to just see them today? It's the Jesus and my mom, Glenda, in me. The "Haley" in me is all Dirty Harry-faced and nothing but business as she strolls through foreign streets in her black knee-high boots, that one half-price professional-ish Dillard's outfit she has worn across the continents, and her lavender backpack strapped around front so you can't get into it behind her. All spice, no sugar.

I received my first lesson in culturally assimilating many years ago during my first trip to New York City during another lifetime. I wore my cute red capris and a great shirt with some splashes of color on it. It was my *I'm-going-to-New-York-and-I'm-cute-outfit*. I walked into the office of my New York City bosses, and one of them looked me up and down and asked what other clothes I brought. I assured her everything else was black. The next day, dressed in black, I greeted everyone who got on the elevator we were riding with a little "good morning" or "hello." I was told, "We don't speak to everyone who gets on the elevator." Noted. Wear black. Don't speak. She was just helping me culturally assimilate. Right? Right.

Today, I'm not wearing red capris and I don't necessarily need my Dirty Harry face as it would be pretty difficult to pick a pocket when everyone is bundled up like Eskimos. I'm wearing my red wool coat that I've realized looks like a Canadian Mountie coat. I'm sure to culturally assimilate wearing this up here in Canada, eh?

This morning's 4 a.m. wakeup call came about 30 minutes after I actually woke up. Tomorrow's wakeup call will be even earlier as we head to the next airport, the next plane, and the next destination. The travel part of this may become a little routine, but the people never do. My heart is already there. I met these friends last year, and I'm so excited to be with them again. These journeys can be a little stressful, but following Jesus wherever He leads is always worth it, and the people I get to call friends change me a little bit at every stop. Sometimes I get a little distracted by the stress of the journey. I really wish I didn't waste that time.

I love this beautiful life and am so very thankful. Sometimes it's stressful. Sometimes it's isolating. Sometimes it's exhausting. I'm not sure why none of my flights can ever be at a time when the sun is already up and that does not leave me feeling a bit like a walking zombie. (I'm just assuming how walking Zombie's feel, and I don't really believe in Zombies.) I've come to know that when I am weak, Christ's strength is more real to me. I will boast in and be thankful for my weakness for just that reason. His grace is always sufficient for me. (2 Corinthians 12:9) I'm not nearly such a boss when I'm tired and cold and have some kind of inner ear/sinus thing happening. But, He, He is a boss. The mountains He moves … I pray wherever you are as you read this, you might stop and ask where He is in your life. Have you looked for Him? See Jeremiah 29:13-14.

I'm at my fun Canadian friend Colleen's house now, smelling crockpot chicken and mashed potatoes. I've already started faking a Canadian accent. It just happens, and I don't know how to stop it. I'm all checked into their guest room and am feeling at home, far away from home. Happy sigh.

Flying into Canada is a lot different than flying into South America where we were just a couple of weeks ago, although I was a little intimidated by the forecasted temperature that had numbers well below zero. It is really cold, but it is still planet Earth.

People are walking around. No one is a frozen statue as soon as they walk outside. Groceries are being bought; coffee is being drunk. Schools are in session. Church doors are open. Cars are driving around with people inside of them. It's just cold. I like it up here.
— *Gracefully Frank*

What's Your Story?

Wherever you are in your walk of faith, think about the people of faith who have gone before you. Maybe the people who made it possible for you to serve where you are in ministry today? Or even the family member(s) you know have prayed for you? Who are they? What did they do, and what do their lives mean to you today?

What in your life is worthy of rejoicing?

Do you know any Canadians? Aren't they fun?

The Inevitable

In all this running around and leaving Tulsa and going to seminary and getting on and off airplanes and crying and laughing and learning and teaching, I turned 40.

Did you ever set goals in life or have some serious expectations that began with the words, "By the time I'm 40?" I did. I had a whole wad of worry that I kept balled up in my fist that made me dread reaching that milestone.

But as soon as I did, my fist just gently relaxed and somehow, the worry lifted up. The boogey man wasn't in the closet or under the bed the night of my birthday. He just wasn't. I did a little unclenching when I turned 40. Who knew that what I had dreaded would bring me so much freedom.

Forty – March 10, 2016

This is my I'm-turning-40 blog. I'm turning 40. Forty-year-old Haley Scully. Did you turn 40 one time? Are you going to turn 40 one day?

I mean, 40. How did this happen? I've been watching my friends turn 40 over these past several months, so it's not like I've had no warning. But, I can't even believe <u>they</u> are 40. I would swear we were just 17. But, I checked my calendar again, and it's coming in six days. Forty. 40. For-T. "How old are you, Haley?" "40." Okay.

It's different than turning 10, 20, or 30, not just in the number of years but also in self-perception and social connotation. At 10, I was all about finally being double digits, Smurfs, rainbows, unicorns. At 20, I was coming out of some really hurtful times; I hardened my resolve and thought, *I'm an adult now and need to act like one*. At 30, I realized, *I'm really an adult now, and it's time to get a handle on some things*.

And now at 40, I no longer have a plan or preconceived notion of how to act. Finally. I know what I know, and I have some ideas about what I don't know. I have so much less figured out than I thought I had before, but there is a Light to my path that I didn't specifically follow before. That Light has a name: Jesus.

I don't know all of the places He will lead, but I am committed to Him. He has inexplicably guided me. I no longer have one foot on, one foot off. He's not just a habit or what I grew up believing. My faith is mine because I sought the Lord with all of my heart, and He was found by me. (Jeremiah 29:13)

I am not looking for a path, a person, a place or a thing to make me who I think I should be. I trust that the Maker of the path is creating me as I take the steps He shows me. I'm a pilgrim in progress, if you will, but not the bonnet-wearing kind of pilgrim.

After three years of first beginning to read John Bunyan's version of the progress of a pilgrim, I'm just now to the part where the Keeper of the Gate let Christiana and Mercy pass through. It's a book worth the attention I'm finally giving it. It's amazing how spot-on it relates to today, though it was written in 1678. "What has been is what will be, and what has been done is what will be done, and there is nothing new under the sun." (Ecclesiastes 1:9, ESV)

However, when one turns the big 4-0, there are some questions that come up, whether you are searching or not. Questions concerning reflection and vision like:

Where have I been?

Where am I going?

Am I doing life right?

Forty doesn't feel like I thought it would. It doesn't look like I thought it would, and I'm pretty sure it doesn't mean what I was once afraid it meant.

It's easy to look at the tangibles, the demographics, the statuses in our lives to try and justify, validate, or prove we are doing life right. We can blame others for what we find, or we give others the glory. We can maybe take a peak around to do a little comparison: "I'm better off than them," or, "I'm worse off than them." We can look at lists we once created to see if we've checked things off. *Have we achieved what is appropriate?*

I'm 40! Does my life matter? Have we made the decisions we needed to make? Have we become everything we wanted to be? Turns out, you can't be anything you dream of being even if you put your mind to it. I'm not Princess Leia. No one has asked me to sing the National Anthem at the Superbowl. I'm not a congresswoman for the great state of Oklahoma (yet). Okay, maybe I haven't really put my mind to those things. My oldest child is not graduating from high school this year. There is no wedding anniversary to celebrate.

But on the flipside, listing all the things I am, have done, or am doing is as fruitless as listing those things I'm not, when considering if I'm doing life right at this 40-year checkpoint.

I've been accepted as many times as rejected, although I tend to focus on one over the other. I'm sure there are more of both to come. I've had successes and failures. Snapshots and spot checks on birthdays don't define a life. Maybe you can relate to some of these questions or thoughts.

Everything I have could be gone tomorrow, or everything I want could show up. Maybe you've lost everything, or maybe you have everything you could ever want. We can compare and compete all day long, but when we finally confess we are not in control and only by God's grace do we live and breathe and move do we come to a place of rest as we turn 40 or any other age. This is me. If comparison and competition aren't my markers for if I'm okay sliding into the big 4-tee, four-ty, forty, what then? "Vanity, vanity . . ."?

In the last few years, I've had to fight hard and dig deep through trials in my life and in my family, as God has given me the opportunity to talk the talk in places I never imagined going. With trials and opportunity come refinement.

To refine and conform me to His image, He keeps leading me to cliffs to trust fall. I DO NOT LIKE TO TRUST FALL. But, He keeps lifting me to new places. He keeps exposing my weaknesses to make me stronger. He keeps making me do, not just be. He keeps increasing my joy. He keeps setting me free. He keeps reminding me of His love right when I need it.

Sometimes I limp down the path He leads me on.
Sometimes He carries me.
But sometimes, I fly.

What I do not have, or what I do have ...
Where I have not been, or where I have been ...

These things don't define me or validate my life at 40. Don't let them define you at any age. That's harder to do when you have everything you want. It's somehow easier to do when you've been left wanting. Both come with perks and disadvantages that we may or may not be aware of.

My life is defined by Jesus Christ. Whoever I am with, wherever I may go, I am His disciple. In plenty or in want, in a crowd, or alone. My life is built on Him. That is what we are made for. I took some time getting here, but it doesn't matter. My rebellion could never overcome His love and faithfulness.

I am also a daughter, a sister, an aunt, a friend. I could be better at all of those, but I find the better I get at being defined by Christ, by His life, by His guidance, the better I get at those other roles.

As I turn 40, I want to be more like Him. I don't want to just act like an adult; I want to live like a Believer. I have said this to friends, so I'll type it out here: my twenties were filled with trying really-really hard to be who I thought I should be. My thirties were filled with gracious tearing down and rebuilding to be who I was made to be. And, my forties … well, I'm about to find out. I am looking forward to this next decade with a faithful and grateful heart.

On my actual birthday, if all goes as planned, I'll wake up in New York City with my two favorite friends who have shared paths with me for almost my whole life. With each step, we have talked out, cried over, prayed through, and laughed about where we have landed. They are my safe place. I'm so glad they turned 40 way-way before me (okay, only months) but that we get to celebrate our birthdays together next week.

Whatever birthday you are coming up on, I pray you would consider what it is you have let define you. In plenty or in want, don't look to the right or to the left. Look up.

In Psalm 138 (NASB) David writes the words in my heart.

I will give You thanks with all my heart;

I will sing praises to You before the gods.

I will bow down toward Your holy temple

And give thanks to Your name for Your lovingkindness and Your truth;

For You have magnified Your word according to all Your name.

On the day I called, You answered me;

You made me bold with strength in my soul.

All the kings of the earth will give thanks to You, O Lord,

When they have heard the words of Your mouth.

And they will sing of the ways of the Lord,

For great is the glory of the Lord.

For though the Lord is exalted,

Yet He regards the lowly,

But the haughty He knows from afar.

Though I walk in the midst of trouble, You will revive me;

You will stretch forth Your hand against the wrath of my enemies,

And Your right hand will save me.

The Lord will accomplish what concerns me;

Your lovingkindness, O Lord, is everlasting;

Do not forsake the works of Your hands.

P.S. All went as planned for Sara, Tiffany, and me. #thiswasforty

– Gracefully Frank

Sara, Me, and Tiffany in Times Square.

What's Your Story?

Have you had any milestone moments or birthdays that you have been tempted to measure your life success by? What was the milestone, and how did you rate yourself?

Are you tempted to look around to see if you are succeeding? In what areas of your life do you find yourself competing or comparing?

Have you looked up to see if you are on the right road according to the One who created you?

Walking in Grace

Have you ever been tempted to think that grace and mercy were given to other people but you had to prove yourself worthy of those things? You have to work harder, be smarter, stay longer, volunteer more, and sleep less?

One of the best things I have had the opportunity to experience more of as I travel through the Sky is <u>grace</u>. When I have no choice but to let go of certain expectations and demands of others or of myself, I have learned how to practice living under conviction not condemnation. There is a big difference in the voice of the Holy Spirit who convicts us toward action and the voice of our enemy who condemns us (guilt trips) toward action. One voice is energizing; the other voice is draining.

I believe you have to listen closely and practice to know the difference. There is a lot of hard work to be done, but, as I walk in grace, it enables me to work smarter, not harder.

There have been times that I have struggled with the difference. I have thought …

Surely, I'm not enough.
Surely, the rest I need is selfish.
Surely, I am a jerk for not serving there, in that way, at that time.

But, the Shepherd's voice is irresistible. When I know it is Him, even when it's something I think I don't want to do, I still want to do it. I keep going wherever He leads because I know it's Him leading. And, when I need grace, mercy, and rest, I accept it and walk in it.

Refreshing Day – July 28, 2016

"Refreshing day." That is what the employees of the conference center where we are staying say as we pass them on the road. At first, I thought maybe it was just a natural thing to say in this African country where I have been for a couple of weeks. But, I found out they say it as part of their hotel slogan. The rainbow, which comes just after a time of refreshing, is a symbol of their parent company. Hence their slogan. It's a symbol of my parent company too. Today, I am taking them both up on a day of refreshing.

The journey I'm on has had me on journey pretty constantly for the past two months. I've loved most every minute. (I was sick for a bit of it after food poisoning in Spain that put me in the ER in OKC, and I've been jet lagged for some of it, so that makes me feel fuzzy and off for at least a week after coming home. I don't necessarily love those parts.) Today, I stepped away from our training conference to have a day of refreshing and preparation. Being able to prepare for the plans ahead next week is very refreshing to me.

I was beginning to get a little panicked thinking about how little time I would have to get ready, but then I realized my teaching time for the current two-day conference could be rescheduled to tomorrow. So, today my training friends and I agreed I could step back, do my laundry, take some time to prepare, and be refreshed.

As my friend/roommate got dressed, I slept in until 7:30 a.m. She left for breakfast, and I made myself some Nescafé in the room. One of those little comforts I am always so excited to see is in-room coffee service. It doesn't always happen, but my heart literally soars when I see a rusty little teapot, some packets of Nescafé, and a coffee cup in the room I've been assigned.

Then I got back in the bed on my side of the night table, propped my pillows just right, sipped a bit of coffee, and opened God's Word. I finished the book of Romans again this morning.

Paul loved the Romans and wanted to get to them so badly, but his journey kept him going other places. He loved and trusted God with His plans, instead of his own.

He really laid out for the Romans the foundation of what he was trying to tell every church he visited or to whom he wrote letters. I think because of his great love for them, and because he wasn't sure when he would see them again, he wanted to make sure the gospel was so clear. The who, what, when, where, how, and why of Jesus can be found in Romans.

Then, after fixing my 2nd cup of Nescafé, I read a few more chapters of an autobiography I've been reading of Pastor Tommy Briggs, whom I will get to work with in another country here in Africa next week. His story has been such an encouragement to me. We have not walked exactly the same road, but our stops have looked somewhat alike.

Then I did laundry. My laundry and I needed this today.

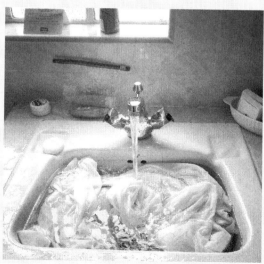

I went for a walk around the campus, stopped in for a little lunch then found a shade tree filled with peacocks to sit under (strategically not under the peacocks) to write a little and be thankful.

Tomorrow I'll be back in the line-up to teach, correct, rebuke, and train (2 Timothy 3:16-17), and I will love it. I feel the most ... well, maybe just put a period after the word "most." I feel the most when I am able to lead people to hope through God's Word and share with them about applying His Word to their everyday life. Not just for the sake of change in their life, but for the sake of who Christ is. The life change, freedom, and heart change is the gracious consequence. He's too much to just tiptoe around trying to follow Him. I want to run after Him until I'm out of breath. I'm all in because of His grace. Grace is a word I didn't understand a lot about growing up. I read a book called *Grace Awakening* by Charles Swindoll that helped me understand it better. If you are looking to understand grace better, that is one I would suggest. I think I have mentioned it before, but it comes to mind again today.

Several days before leaving for this trip, I returned home from a multi-week trip to Thailand and Indonesia. We attended a pastor conference in Bangkok. We enjoyed one sightseeing day in Thailand before traveling to Indonesia to spend seven days with our ministry partners there. Seven days, five hotels, five flights, 100's of beautiful faces, and many sweet friends. Out of 20 days, we had two days totally off from our work to enjoy sightseeing on our own tab. These are days of picture taking (something I love to do) and grabbing the occasional something-to-remember this by souvenir.

The pictures I share are usually from these few days. It is rare that I share the faces or stories of the people I serve with in my blog. I'm not really the authorized teller of their stories outside of the ministry where I serve. But, I am the one to tell my story. I stand amazed by what God is doing, and I am grateful for His gifts. God is good. He is refreshing.

In the midst of the work He has given me, He gives me sunsets, water taxies, Chicken Pad Thai next to the Bridge on The River Kwai, ginger tea in Ubud, and today: Nescafé and peacocks.

– *Gracefully Frank*

Water taxis at a market in Bangkok.

My cup of ginger tea at the rice fields in Ubud, Indonesia.

Several years ago a movie was made from a book that had been written by a woman who went out to find meaning in her life by eating and praying and loving. While we were in Indonesia, our friends planned to take us to Ubud, which happened to be the place in the book where the author found love.

Before we left our hotel that morning, I pulled up the day's news on my phone. I found that on that same day we were to visit Ubud, the author, and the love she had found there, had filed for divorce.

It struck me that I would be in that place on that day. So many people had been inspired by her story. Many readers of her book set out on similar journeys, wanting the same inspiration, adventure, and happy ending. I had watched the movie, and even though I hard rolled my eyes a couple of times, I found myself longing for the passionate love she found in Ubud. I have no idea about the particulars of their marriage or how it ended, and in no way am I making a comment on their personal life, but I do think I have some credibility to comment on the message of the book as I've had some opportunity to see and taste the places she shared. It's not that her whole journey unraveled with the end of her marriage, but the happily-ever-after part that she sold to millions of people apparently did.

If we take anything from her bold and fascinating story, maybe it should be …

Eat.

Pray to the One True God who can hear you.

Love that is eternal has a name: it's Jesus.

What's Your Story?

Think of times that you have listened to the voice of conviction that helped you make a healthy or wise decision, and think of times that you have heard the voice of condemnation making you feel shame or discouraged. Have you ever stopped to think about the difference? Which voice have you most often followed?

What are the small delights in your life that even in the busiest or stressful seasons you find comfort and joy?

Are you truly praying to God, considering who He is and what His promises are, and asking Him for His guidance? Or, might you just be sitting still, being quiet, and thinking thoughts but not putting them into action?

Confirmation

You know how some things only work in very specific places under very specific circumstances? Like how a tornado only forms if the winds wrap up just right and something about wind sheers and vortexes and converging warm and cold fronts and cloud to ground something or other happens? It takes very specific circumstances to make a tornado.

Jesus does not take a very specific set of circumstances in order to happen. He happens everywhere. In some places, here in America and elsewhere around the world, the message of Jesus gets presented in terms of achieving certain levels of prosperity: that a person has to line up very specific circumstances in order to receive Him. And, if they do it just right, they'll please Him enough to get Him.

I realize my own desire for Land was actually sort of buying into this concept of who God should be and what He should do for me if I am obedient. The hope of prosperity works a bit like a pyramid scheme with the proclaimer of it receiving the most benefit. Then, they present their riches as evidence back at those who paid for them as proof that they are doing something right. When, actually, it's just proof that they are master manipulators.

In many parts of the world, a person can't just believe and achieve wealth. The conditions are not available everywhere to live an American Dream or what some people may consider would be their "best life now." It looks really silly taking that message into places torn apart by war and devastated by natural or man-made disasters. The distortion of a gospel for prospering falls on ears that have been deafened long ago because it looks like some concept of America, not like their homeland, and definitely not like Christ.

It is a great tragedy when that message of prosperity is tied to the gospel of Jesus Christ because it is not sustainable beyond certain borders. Hope seems impossible, and the people feel forsaken. I love America, but it's Christ I take to the nations, not my colonial ideas of what would be good for them denominationally or socio-economically. Those concepts don't apply everywhere. Jesus does. If you can't take the message you are pushing into every hut and home and it make sense, then the message you are pushing is not the true Good News for humanity. It is not the gospel of Jesus.

I've had those mind-twisting thoughts, wondering what God is doing for people born into other faiths and in Lands where His Word hasn't reached. *Is it reasonable to say that one Son of God could be the Savior of the entire world?* The Bible speaks to all of these questions. Many times though, we ask our questions into the wind instead of into His Word.

The more I read His Word, the more I understand and also the more I realize that I won't fully understand all the answers to all the questions. But unmistakably, the hope of His true gospel works everywhere.

"Many times though, we ask our questions into the wind instead of into His Word."

I've seen that confirmation in the faces of Believers on five of the seven continents. They don't all speak the same language. They don't all sing the same songs. They don't all pray the same way. The circumstances are very different, but Jesus is very much the same.

In every place, for every heart, the gospel of Jesus Christ applies. The way God is getting that message to people born in other places is through us. We are the messengers.

Since the beginning of this journey, with that first trip to Israel, I've been in many countries and met with literally thousands of people from all walks of life and backgrounds.

Some born into other faiths.
Some born into peace.
Some born into war.
Some born into privilege.
Some born into poverty.

The true gospel of Jesus Christ applies to them whether they sit in a hut, a home, or a high-rise.

Following – November 11, 2016

Over the past few months, I've traveled new streets, alleys, subways, stairways on mountainsides, beaches, and aisles in various places around Asia. I've walked beside friends who speak different languages but are of the same heart, and walked past strangers with the only resemblance being our humanity.

Smells of fish markets, sewage, incense, and flowers; sights of tall buildings, small shacks, sweet smiles, blank stares, bright colors, and filth have all swirled around in my thoughts. We have been to places where women are treated like cattle and places where cattle are treated as gods. Some of these places are beautiful; others are barren. These contrasts of people and places are as consistent as the similarities.

Everywhere we go, people are following. They are following their culture, their heritage, and their religious or non-religious ideologies. Some are following their passions, their educational opportunities, or their chance for freedom. No one is sitting still. Every person, even the lame and the beggars on the sides of roads, are following whatever system has been laid before them. We like to think we are autonomous, but we govern ourselves within the concepts we have been offered. We all follow what we have been taught, what we have believed, or what we have experienced.

In many of the places we have visited, people have been taught to follow various religions. Humanity is made to seek a purpose in life, and we seem to have a habit of creating to-do lists in the hopes of finding a good one. Some people seek everything but God, in a sort of protest to those they think represent Him.

There are so many life plans that could be followed. I've seen people who follow their ancestors into temples with images carved by man, where birds nest and desecrate, and where the god they serve is silent. People follow celebrities, prophets, and regimes. In many places, people have little choice but to follow the cultural or religious expectations of them based on caste, gender, or birth order. People are often tempted to follow popularity as if popularity equals truth and purpose.

The plans for living and rules for religion are so drastically different. I could never comprehend, debate, or convince someone born in a reality so different than mine, whether they live in my state or on another continent, to view the world, or God, as I do.

Thankfully, convincing is not my job. Sharing the message so that others are presented the same option I've been given and chosen, and representing that well with my life, is my job. Once the message is shared, there is another voice there to convince, and my life is only one testimony in a very large ocean of testimonies.

Here are two things I've found that strengthen my faith instead of proving it false in all these different places: 1) God's Word is always proven true. 2) There is one common voice that can be heard above all the issues and expectations of this life no matter the location. It's a consistent voice that speaks to those seeking God, no matter where they were born. It's not a cool voice from the nightly news that resounds around the world. No government official, celebrity, or even preacher (except maybe Billy Graham) has a voice that resonates across cultures and continents. The lives of people recovering from an earthquake, a woman rescued from slavery, a child who lost parents, the sick, the brokenhearted, the lonely, are not transformed by an enlightening or witty tweet. Those who met Jesus in their dreams, chose to follow Him, and are now desperate to keep their lives out of fear that even their own family member may kill them, have little concern about getting likes on social media.

The voice unites us; issues do not unite us. Issues are like plays on a stage where the curtain will eventually come down. We can get so wrapped up in a scene that we forget to plan where we are going when it's over. It's good to get into the scenes where we live and work together, but issues are geographically and socioeconomically confined. They can be a temporal distraction from the eternal real issue for humanity: salvation through the Messiah, Jesus.

Jesus, true Jesus, comes with a voice that unites people across all boundaries, plans, and presumptions. Respectfully, if you say that isn't true, then you haven't been hearing Him. You have been listening to other voices. Many say they represent His voice, but their hate and their selfishness prove otherwise. Others claim to represent Him, but their complete disregard for His Word for the proclaimed sake of tolerance or kindness, as the enemy has twisted these definitions, proves their hearts otherwise. Jesus teaches us to view the world as He does and reveals to us more about who He is through His Word and one another. Following Him is the only plan that has consistent relevance in the gutters of India, the high-rises of Hong Kong, and the streets of America.

It's amazing to me that people can follow Him the same way in such different places, even though He did tell us in His Word that we would recognize His voice, follow Him, and that He would know us. (John 10:27) It's still amazing to see this similarity of purpose, this same path, and same Shepherd followed by pastors in the Himalayas of Asia and mothers in the Serengeti of Africa. It's that voice that my friends on completely different continents, with completely different life circumstances, have heard.

Their unity of vision and purpose and heart is miraculous. Many people I've met cannot even consider the Western concept of impacting change on their government or social standing through education or elections. Where options are so few, things become so clear. His voice has so much less competition. Our human hope cannot be in anything that is irrelevant to some of us, or only applicable to a few of us. With all the exclusivity we see, only Jesus is all inclusive. Respectfully, if you do not see that, you are looking at someone other than Him.

He does expect us to follow Him though. It is not supposed to be the other way around, no matter how entitled we may think we are. He spans all time and eternity. He sees the big picture of creation. It takes faith to choose Him, and steps of faith can be hard to take. When you find Him faithful, though, the next steps of faith are taken alongside experience. The steps get easier and easier. I can testify. Faith plus experience equals confidence.

When I am tempted with doubt, when I wonder where He is, when others reject or ignore my value (or yours), He is near. He is near the souls I have met these past few months. He loves the same, His Word is the same, and His voice is the same. That can't always be said of those of us who follow Him, but it can always be said of Him. He never changes geographically or socioeconomically.

Generations see either the blessing of those who follow the Lord, or they see the depravity of those who do not follow Him. This has been told to us in His Word (Exodus 34:6-7, for instance) and confirmed everywhere I've been. I haven't been everywhere, but God has made the way for me to see 29 countries in these past five years, with number 30 coming this weekend.

I always pray to understand what He is teaching me, to share what I believe, what I've learned, what I've experienced. Our lives are not our own; they are for His glory. His blessing as we follow Him is as constant as the removal of His blessing when we choose to disregard Him. Many of us have seen that too.

He is the blessing, and with Him comes increasing joy, love, peace, patience, kindness, goodness, faithfulness, gentleness, and self-control. Who you follow matters. It matters today and tomorrow and the next tomorrow. Everyone is following someone. Someone is probably following you. Where are you taking them?

— *Gracefully Frank*

What's Your Story?

Ask yourself, and seek an honest answer, who are you following? Whose back is right in front of you? Who are you trying to be more like? Who are you trying to please?

Who is following you?

Where are you taking them?

You Should ...

How many sentences begin with those words? "You should ..."
Have you ever heard that? You should ...

go to church,
try my hairstylist,
listen to this new song,
break up with him,
go to that new Chinese place,
read this new book,
exercise,
eat more vegetables,
call your mom,
put yourself out there,
try harder,
give yourself a break,
try this recipe.

We say and hear "you should" a lot. So how do we know if we should or not? We should try suggestions out for ourselves. You should check out what God has for you in your Sky, wherever that may be for you. I've said before that we shouldn't try to wear someone else's shoes, but in this next blog post I just merely suggest trying a pair on.

Lemon Cake and Used Shoes – April 07, 2017

How do you know if that recipe you just downloaded for the best lemon cake on the planet really is? Could it be a better recipe than the one you already have? How can you know it's not? Sometimes we have really strong opinions about things that we haven't even baked for ourselves. I'm not trying to climb up in your oven, but maybe it's time to turn it on and do a little baking.

I have this recipe ... If you don't want to try my recipe for yourself, maybe you will consider slipping into my shoes for a minute and see what is happening. This recipe, these shoes, this God who is faithful – in fact, the point of every word I write – you should try following Him. Maybe if you put on my used shoes, you might get a feel for how this cake tastes.

Recipe:

Read the Bible every day. You may have heard OF Him, but you can read the Bible to hear FROM Him.

- Just start somewhere. Ask God to help you understand.
- Download the "YouVersion" Bible app that has so many different ways you can start or the "Read Scripture" app which is

one of my favorites. Or just dust off the Bible on your shelf and consider starting in the Gospel of John.

- I write out whatever passage I'm reading in the morning because I like to write with a pen on paper. Like taking notes, it helps me process.
- Then I write what questions I had, or I write down what stuck out to me. It's part of a morning conversation over coffee. Have I mentioned before I like coffee and conversation?

Listen to what you read. Watch how it applies. Do what you learn.

There will be ways to apply His Word in your daily life that will help you through decisions, sorrows, joys. Then, you can share how you are encouraged with someone else to help them in their decisions, sorrows, joys.

Be changed, in a good way. Don't read to be smart; read to be real. Read to live it.

This world is difficult to understand. When we are confused, we often wonder where God is and what He is doing. Hearing soundbites and blurbs don't help you know His Word or Him any better. Reading the Bible helps us know Him more. I shouldn't really comment on Harry Potter books because I've never read those books. So how do I know if they are great or not? How do you know Jesus, or His Word, if you have not read it for yourself?

Have you baked this recipe before? You should try it. This recipe gave me the strength to walk the walk I'm walking in the shoes I've been given.

My Used Shoes:

Two weeks ago, I was boarding my first flight of the year. Our travel path took us straight south, in the same time zone, and we would only be gone a week. I was excited that it seemed like a light schedule. On our way to Mexico, my playlist played through to "It Is Well" by Bethel Music.

"So let go my soul and trust in Him

The waves and wind still know His name …"

I didn't feel a heaviness on my heart that day as we flew through the Sky, but, the song was sinking deep into me so I hit the repeat button. For the remainder of the flight, I listened to it over and over.

We arrived in Mexico, and on the car ride to the hotel we were told that the number of attendees we had planned to join in a small room the next morning had tripled and we had been moved to a new venue. (My instant go-to insecure thoughts: *my clothes are dumb, and I'm not ready for a larger audience. I talk with my hands too much for more people to join us. Someone real should've come.*) The words of the song from that day came back to my mind: "Let go my soul and trust in Him. The waves and wind still know His name." The song I didn't need, I all of a sudden needed.

There was no coffee and it wasn't morning, but I had a conversation with Him about it. *Ok. So, what you have prepared for me to share is the same in a small room as in a big room, but the responsibility seems to have tripled. But, I know you are not punking or cheating them by sending me. It's never me. It's always you. Whatever you spoke to their heart to bring them here, you are faithful, and you will do it. I will be as confident in the small room as the big room because you are my confidence. Not my dumb skirt. Not my over-exaggerated hand motions as I act out the words I speak. You. I was expecting calm seas. Run down here to Mexico and knock it out. Manageable in my mind. But, the wind has kicked up, and there are waves. What if I sink? I came here thinking I was doing this <u>for</u> you, but find myself in desperate need <u>of</u> you, again and again and again. Thank you for every moment that reminds me of this. Through it all my eyes are on you, and it is well with me.*

The next morning I woke up, made a double instant Folgers travel packet coffee with my plug-in heating element and a borrowed cup and saucer from the restaurant, and got my Bible out to hear from Him. I've been in Luke. Going through pieces of each chapter each day, writing it out. That morning in Mexico, I picked up where I had left off the day before.

This is the story it happened to be:

> *"One day he got into a boat with his disciples, and he said to them, 'let us go across to the other side of the lake.' So they set out, and as they sailed he fell asleep. And a windstorm came down on the lake, and they were filling with water and were in danger. And they went and woke him, saying 'Master, Master, we are perishing!' And he awoke and rebuked the <u>wind</u> and the raging <u>waves</u>, and they ceased, and there was a calm. He*

said to them, 'Where is your faith?' And they were afraid, and they marveled, saying to one another, 'Who then is this, that he commands even winds and water, and they obey him?'" (Luke 8:22-25, ESV)

OOOkaaay. Really? Yesterday the song hung in my spirit: today that very passage is here for me. It took the obedience of being in His Word, beginning in Luke weeks ago, to get the blessing of His Word on this day. *Where is your faith, Haley?* It's right there in Jesus' boat. In that song. In that Scripture. In my Savior. And, it's growing still.

This is what it is like when, as Christians, we talk about Christ never leaving nor forsaking us. This is what it is like to "do life" with Jesus. This is a very practical example of how God works in us when we seek Him. The blessing comes in nurturing the relationship.

The song He stuck in my head the day before, He spoke to my heart the morning of. Ready to apply it, because I had read it, heard it, and believed it. Kind of like when you follow the recipe for the best lemon cake on the planet … you get cake. No one can make you bake it, but you should.

If you don't listen, you won't hear. If you don't read His Word, you won't experience Him fully. If you don't seek Him, you won't find Him. If you don't taste, you won't see. I won't either.

I went to that big room that morning excited, not anxious. The waves and wind were calmed by His voice. *What was He going to do in that place?* I wanted to be part of it. *What was He going to do that He would speak to even my heart?* I was excited to see. In a room that grew smaller with each moment that we spent together, Jesus made the best lemon cake.

When the waves and the wind were over, we spent some lovely moments growing deeper in love with the people and the place. I took some pictures along the journey. Following Him is my favorite.

— Gracefully Frank

Blending in at Chichen Itza in Mexico.

Waving goodbye to my gracious friends.

What's Your Story?

Do you get tired of people telling you, "you should?" Consider whether it is wisdom, stubbornness, hurt, or maybe fear that keeps you from following their encouragement.

Have you considered trying the recipe included in this chapter?

Have you ever sought Scripture to guide your steps or found a certain passage that speaks exactly to what you are going through that day? Do you consider it a coincidence or a blessing? Why?

... But, Not Lost

The Sky has been a surprising place for me. Letting go and lifting up, I thought I would be giving up so much of what I always wanted. But, the Sky has taken me to places that my heart longed for without me even knowing it. The desires of my heart have been fulfilled in so many ways as I fly through the Sky going from Land to Land.

Wandering — July 03, 2017

I woke up just before my alarm went off at 3 a.m. this morning, and I was so glad it didn't jar me out of a dead sleep. It's always better when I'm able to drift back awake. As soon as I opened my bedroom door, the smell of Folger's classic roast hit me in the face. I was thankful for a coffee pot that can be programmed the night before.

What an unnecessary and wonderful invention. I filled the cup (also planned the night before) and went back to a little table with an old lamp and half burnt candle to open the Word that would give me strength for this day and, undoubtedly the days to come.

The ribbon bookmark was holding the page for Luke 20:41-47. Jesus answered a lot of questions with questions. Although He knew the answers to the questions, He chose to respond to the motives of the person/people who were doing the asking. He knew why they asked. He knew what they were trying to get at. He knew when it was hurt, fear, doubt, or pride that motivated their questions. He's still good at that. He knows why we have questions. He's not afraid to answer them as He reveals our motives and calms and heals the sometimes thinly-veiled heart of our question.

Reading Luke's letter to a man named Theophilus to explain what and who Jesus was and is, is a great place to watch what Jesus did and why. If a respected doctor you knew wrote you a letter about some pretty amazing things that were going on, would you read it? Would you save it? Would you share it? Theophilus did.

That was all I wrote of this blog, as I sat in the OKC airport waiting for my first liftoff. Now, I'm at the conclusion of this trip as I type this from window seat 25A, pointed against the wind toward the east coast of America. Sixteen days feels a lot longer than it looks on the little calendar on my phone. It usually does when I'm so far from home.

My first stop was to meet up with a colleague, who has become a good friend after several years of working and traveling together. Our planes from different countries landed thirty-minutes apart in an old city in Europe where I never imagined going and now have been several times.

I know what train to get on for the city center, which Cathedral is my favorite, and where to get an amazing cup of coffee in a beautiful little pot. No one there recognizes me or knows my name, but I know my own little bit about their city.

Our walk-around plan prior to our next flight was cut short after some undesired but welcome intel from our global security partners. We stayed a full day in our hotel room out of an abundance of caution, but it was good to have a little extra time to nap off jet lag before the next leg of the journey and practice resting in His peace.

We left Europe for Central Asia where more friends with multiple accents, cultures, and histories gathered. It was the first time to have plans with one set of accents. At the conclusion of four days together, hope and friendships had grown.

One man said he did not know I was a woman when he agreed to join us for three days of training, and he was disappointed on our first day to find me as such. He has been a shepherd of people for many years and said he did not think learning from me would be possible. "But," he said with a smile, "this week has proven that with God all things are possible." *gulp*

God has led me to lay down many notions in many nations, and I appreciated

"God has led me to lay down many notions in many nations ..."

his gracious frankness. God is more than we think and faithful to accomplish everything He says He will do. He was faithful to me and my friends, for our good and His glory. *Then. Sings. My. Soul.*

We had one day off between groups. I took two naps during what was a more-than-welcomed rainy day. Then we began five days with a different set of accents that I've come to be familiar with over the last several years. I still cannot begin to comprehend their words or their lives. But, I know Who knows them. He brings us together to share a few moments of our lives with each other. It's a mystery to me, but, being convinced of His presence, His power, and His goodness, we come together in His name. *No. Turning. Back.*

My friends with many accents have lots of questions, and in our moments together God gives us a special freedom to discuss. Our conversations are a safe place to pose some lingering, sometimes previously unspoken, thoughts. I've asked a lot of questions over the years too. I've asked *who* and *what* and *when* and *where* and *how.* I've debated. I've tried to trap God with his own Word: "But you said, so shouldn't you ..." I've reasoned. I've thought I was so smart, so logical, until these recent years when I dug in, began letting go, and committed to stop asking so many questions and just start saying *yes.*

Sometimes saying yes has led me to be hurt, rejected, and ignored. I sneak a few questions in during those times. *Why again, God?* My life does not fit into any reasonable (in my understanding) box, and sometimes, even in my gratitude, that makes me feel like such a weirdo.

I think Jesus knows my motive when I ask Him why. Whether hurt, fear, doubt, or pride, He seems to be more interested in my heart and motives than answering my questions. As He forms my inner being from one degree of glory to the next, my momentary questions take a backseat to my resolve to trust this Shepherd who is my one constant. I have so little to give. Only my whispered, sometimes anxious, "yes," but then He tears down walls and grows gardens out of the rubble. When I take my eyes off Him I sink like a rock into doubt. But when my eyes are on Him …

I see mountains and oceans and
tears and smiles and
Lands and Sky.
I hear hearts and accents
and whispers of the way to walk (Isaiah 20:21)
and praise worship.
He gives so much with just a yes.
Which then convinces me to give the next yes.

On my way home this time, He gave me a wee bit of Ireland. Two and a half days with my friend to walk where streets do have names in Dublin. To ride a big Touristy McTouristan tour bus across the isle to see the Cliffs of Moher and Galway and green and rocks and rain and blue sky.

I've dreamed of going to Ireland since I was a little girl and always requested bedtime stories about rainbows and leprechauns.

Deep in my gut, there has always been a wanting to go back to the land where my grandpa's grandpa, Thomas Scully, left home and country to come to America.

I learned a lot more about the potato famine and the struggle for Catholics like my great-great-Grandpa Thomas during the mid-1800s and what may have led him to leave. Whatever he hoped for his generations to come as he left, I hope a piece of that was realized as I arrived back there this week. Either in his desperation or courage, or probably both, he did us good. And though no one there knew, I carried his name and blood back to that rocky soil. I usually leave pieces of my heart on each Land I step, but in Ireland, I found pieces of my heart already there waiting for me.

Below you will find a few pictures as I continue to document this journey. For so many years there were no pictures of my life as it seemed to me there was nothing to note. I had such specific ideas of what was noteworthy. I often took pictures for other people, of their families and babies and lives. The enemy of my soul had me so wrapped up in distrust and disappointments to distract me from the beauty of the life I have been given. It's not that now I have pictures to take because there are more places and faces in my life; rather, I have more pictures to take because in changing my heart the Lord drastically changed my ideas of what is noteworthy. That change in gratitude literally opened up the world for me to be grateful. Maybe still a bit of weirdo to my own set of well-founded, very logical cultural expectations, but, a weirdo on purpose because I consider Him faithful who promised to have plans for me in following Him.

(Jeremiah 29:11) Not because of who I am, but because of who He is.

He knows my name,

and He knows your name.

He is the same for me as He is for you.

It just depends on whether or not we are willing to say yes or if we allow the trees to block our view of the beautiful forest before us.
— *Gracefully Frank*

Out the tour bus window as we left Dublin.

At the Cliffs of Moher doing my very best Mary Kate Danaher impersonation.

Street band in Galway.

Coffee in Dublin.

What's Your Story?

What questions do you have about Jesus? Whom could you ask?

Has saying "yes" to God ever led you to be hurt or rejected? Have you talked about that with anyone? Have you been able to see the good in that situation?

What in your life is noteworthy and picture worthy? Will you share your pictures with others? Pictures of your marriage, your children, your ministry, your Bible, your best friend, your quiet spot, cup of coffee, rainy day, sunny day, furry friend.

Part 4:

Promised Landing

Haley L. Scully

Therefore

In 2014, the Ponca City Senior High School Class of 1994 celebrated their 20th Class Reunion. That's my class and man I like them. I had a moment with a classmate and her son as we stood in line for Snyder's fried chicken at our Ponca Lake family picnic that stayed in my mind.

She introduced me to her young son as a "world-traveler." He looked at me, and his eyes kind of got wide as he said, "Cooool." Flashbacks of how un-cool I am flooded my mind, and I really wanted to sit down and explain to them the behind-the-scenes story, and tell them about Who the cool One really is.

If people only see the surface – the blogs from Nepal or the Instagram pictures from Zambia – but never know the depths of what God has done to get me there, it can be easy to confuse who the story is about and from where the power comes.

I have been in many leadership roles even since elementary school, and I have always enjoyed being a part of programs, solutions, and scenes. But, if only the highlight reel is visible, then I could be a distraction. It's the lowlights that need to be told in order for the story to have full life and His glory to be revealed. I have to share my insecurities, fears, pride, and failures as *gracefully frank* as I can muster the courage to share them.

If people see me, the "world traveler," then I have failed to share the story well. If they see Jesus as someone they want to know better because of the salvation, healing, and purpose He gives, even to an angry chicken like me, then I've told the story more clearly.

People may have seen me as a leader at times, but they possibly didn't see me when I've been broken and afraid because I certainly never wanted to share that side of who I was as readily as I wanted to share my successes. But, God knew my broken pieces. We don't all have to get out and confess those, but this is something in particular He has asked me to do through this journey.

I make them known, to make Him known.

My story isn't one of past sexual or physical abuse or trauma that I overcame. I do not have previous addictions to sex, drugs, or alcohol, although there were certainly witnesses to my sins that saw weaknesses in all of these areas. Many powerful testimonies of the Lord come through terrible hurts and healings such as those, but, by His grace, I cannot relate to the level of pain in those redemptions.

I grew up in a safe home, although nowhere near perfect, on a nice street in the best state in the United States of America. My great battle has not been a physical war, it has been a war whispered in my ear by a snake. "Where is God?" "Where is your blessing?" "You are all alone." "He isn't taking care of you." "Is He even real?"

There have been broken and painful relationships, disappointments, betrayals, and rejections that set me on some of the courses I've chosen. God knows the path He has allowed in my life and all that He protected me from, and all that He brought me through, to get me where He had planned for me.

One day in Branson, when the flood broke loose and fear took hold of me deep down in that cave (okay, actually down only the first flight of stairs, but down in that cave), a new course of life began. I was given the choice to stay where I was, begging for Land, or choose to rise and fly through the Sky.

Christ gave me the strength to rise. Just an ordinary person who said yes to our extraordinary Savior. Even with feet dragging, He has transformed me just as His Word promises. That is who He is and what He will do.

"After this there was a feast of the Jews; and Jesus went up to Jerusalem. Now there is at Jerusalem by the sheep market a pool, which is called in the Hebrew tongue Bethesda, having five porches. In these lay a great multitude of impotent folk, of blind, halt, withered, waiting for the moving of the water. For an angel went down at a certain season into the pool, and troubled the water: whosoever then first after the troubling of the water stepped in was made whole of whatsoever disease he had. And a certain man was there, which had an infirmity thirty and eight years. When Jesus saw him lie, and knew that he had been now a long time in that case, he saith unto him, Wilt thou be made whole? The impotent man answered him, Sir, I have no man, when the water is troubled, to put me into the pool: but while I am coming, another steppeth down before me. Jesus saith unto him, Rise, take up thy bed, and walk. And immediately the man was made whole, and took up his bed, and walked: and on the same day was the Sabbath." (John 5:1-9, KJV)

First of all, I had to add the words "saith" and "steppeth" into

Microsoft Word's dictionary; also note that the word "impotent" has more than one meaning.

Next of all, many of us are laying poolside: struggling, trying, frustrated, waiting, blaming, broken. *Sir, I have no man* ... or ...*another steppeth down before me.* We think like the lame man beside the pool ... if only people were fair and honored the line instead of walking into the waters ahead of him. If only someone would lend him a hand. All of this man's "if onlys" were dependent on the actions of others. He lay there, crippled for "thirty and eight years" waiting for fairness and a leg up. Fair didn't come. Rational, respectable help from his neighbors didn't come. But, the Savior did.

The man expected healing to come in the water, and he kept waiting for someone to help him into it. Healing came when he believed Jesus and then acted on his belief, otherwise known as faith.

That's when my healing came, too. Where are you expecting healing to come from? Many of us sit on the side of the pool waiting and complaining and annoyed or scared that things do not change, and yet we never see that it is us whose unwillingness to change keeps us laid out on our bed watching the Land we desire, and the healing we need, stay beyond our reach. We sometimes act insulted to consider that we should have to change anything. But, the Savior is walking by. Will you hold to excuses, or rise and walk? Maybe even rise and fly.

Jesus didn't get down and talk for hours with the twisted up man, coaxing him into healing. Basically, He said do it or don't. It's right here for you. "Wilt thou be made whole?" Yes or no? Stay there, or, "Rise, take up your bed, and walk." Lift. Let go of what is strangling you, depressing you, frustrating you, or distracting you, and rise.

This man could have tried to demand

"Healing came when he believed Jesus and then acted on his belief, otherwise known as faith."

that Jesus lower him into the water for the healing that he wanted so badly and had expected all along. I could continue to demand that Jesus heal me in all the ways I think healing should come. I could sit and demand Land, or I could rise.

Maybe you have your Land and aren't even looking for the Savior. Maybe you believe you have life all handled on your own and you don't see anyone ahead of you leading the way. If all conditions (health, wealth and weather) stay the same then it may be difficult for you to see your need. Unfortunately, health, wealth, and weather very rarely all stay the same.

Who you follow matters, and who you are waiting on matters.

What's Your Story?

What is your testimony of redemption? Have you sought or accepted Christ as your Savior?

Has Jesus been telling you to rise in one way, but you are still looking for healing to come in another?

Land Redefined

Most of my life, I looked for a place to Land, until God gave me a taste for the Sky.

Many of the things that I have been most afraid of, I have been given opportunity to walk through.

Being alone used to be my greatest fear.
Being unloved was a heartbreaking thought.
Being unimportant kept me working to prove myself constantly.
I've been all of those things.

Cancer diagnosis in people I love, happened. I've turned 30 and even 40 without a husband or children. I've been rejected and ignored by people I admired and loved. The things of this earth that I longed for to recognize God's blessing have often vanished as clocks have ticked and people have walked away from me or I have had to walk away from them. I don't have the traditional blessed life that many of us look for as we think of growing up and growing old. But as my heart grew darker, the Lord Himself walked by the pool and told me to rise. Then, *in the light of His face, the things of earth began to grow strangely dim ...* and as I let Him lift me through the clouds that I was so afraid of, life began to shine again.

He has not filled me how I had longed to be filled; He chose instead to heal me from pain that kept me fighting with Him. He whispered louder to me than my enemy could ever muster enough voice to overcome. He began the work to change my heart from one that was growing cold and sick to one set free to fly.

I was so afraid to consider a life that looked like anything other than what I knew or understood, until He led me to walk through exactly the life I feared He would hold me to:

A life lived for Him, and not for myself. His will, not mine. His will is better because He knows a lot more than I do.

He did this not to hurt me, but to set me free. He did this to give me His presence. His love. His purpose. His Land and Sky. He pursued me so that I could tell you about Him. It doesn't require being single and childless to live totally for God and not for yourself. It's just what has been required of me.

I would be lying if I said all other hopes have vanished in the blissful joy of walking with Him. There are times when I wish I was writing about knowing God in deeper ways because of loving my husband. I cannot write about my experiences of being a mommy and raising children who eat healthy, make good grades, and will one day change the world. There are no family pictures standing in a wheat field with clothes of coordinating hues and knee high boots with one of my children making a silly face. (Maybe I've thought about that a few times.) I do have a few Crockpot recipes I'm pretty proud of, but I found them on other people's blogs and had nothing to do with their creation.

My name is Haley Lougene Scully.

I'm 42.

I am not a wife.

I am not a mother.

I am not Paleo.

I am not a diffuser.

But, I am chosen.

It took me a long time to believe that last point is true in spite of how I expected life to turn out. I had to quit waiting for proof I could recognize and rise, take up my mat, and start walking in the truth until I could see it.

Marriage and children are very obviously God's great blessing throughout His Word. Two are better than one. Generations to follow you are His gifts of this life. But they cannot be the sole purpose of it. They still come in second to the greatest Gift.

I've served with followers of Christ in countries where generations of men have been killed. There are places where these blessings of family are physically impossible to obtain. So what does that say if we believe God's hand of favor comes in the form of the American Dream family portrait? Where God has taken me has changed my view and expectations of how His goodness should appear.

God's hand of favor came in the form of Jesus. All of us have access to Him – whether we live in a village in Tanzania, a high-rise in Hong Kong, an apartment in Turkey, or a little red brick house with 10 feral cats in the yard in Oklahoma. I am not trying to elevate singleness or lessen marriage. *By no means!* I am saying that both can be beautiful if lived in His grace and purpose. Seek Him first, and let Him write the story.

On that note, however, if you know a guy, feel free to orchestrate an introduction. #jokingnotjoking People have asked me if I feel called to singleness. I wish I could say yes so there would be some kind of grand justification for not being married. But, I don't feel called to singleness; I feel called to Christ. I do not put how, when, or what God will do with that in a box anymore: marriage or singleness. I am the most focused on faithfulness to Him. I'm not being faithful to Him so that He will bring me my Land and husband. I'm faithful to Him because He is God.

So far, where He has led, as He has supplied all of my needs, marriage has not been a part of the story He has written. I live in a hopeful expectation of His faithfulness, based on my experiences, that He does indeed have plans. He will show His plans to me when the time is right and then He will be faithful to complete them, whether or not that includes marriage. I definitely don't want to encourage people to define who they are based on their marital status. I'm going to follow Jesus and let Him decide where we go.

The Lord has given me Land in 33 countries so far where I have held hands with, cried with, and prayed with my family in Christ. It took giving me the Sky, that I never wanted, to get to the incredible Land that He had for me.

The presence of ache for Land no longer envelops the joy of the Sky. I would not go back. I would not wake up from this life and hope to find anything that would undo the love and faith I have in Him now. Each day, I live through experiences of His faithfulness and am learning not to try to work everything out according to my plan, but to trust that He will work all things for my good.

This trust has eternally grounded me in Him.
He is my Land.
Land has been redefined.

The moment that I let go of the Land clenched in my fists is the moment my wings began to grow. I pray that in sharing the story of His amazing faithfulness, you will be prompted to look up and see the Sky He is painting for you and that you will walk humbly and lightly on the Land beneath your feet. Seek Him, and follow His lead.

Be steadfast as you travel down the bumpy runway of following Him. Just keep doing the next right thing in His direction.

Maybe that next right thing is asking a friend to have coffee and talk about some of your questions.

Maybe that is going to a Bible study someone has invited you to attend.

Maybe that is going to church for the first time, or going *back* to church for the first time in a long time.

Maybe that is downloading one of those Bible apps and beginning each day in His Word.

I don't know what that looks like for you specifically, but He does. He'll show you. Ask Him. He is a game changer, and many of us need our game changed. Anticipate bumps as you lift off and begin to rise but also know that a pretty incredible view awaits you. When you touch back down to the Land where He leads, you may find yourself standing right where you began ... but with a whole new heart to feel it and eyes to see the beauty in it.

What's Your Story?

How have you defined Land?

How have you looked at singleness either in your own life, or in the life of others?

Do you think you possibly need to re-think some of your thoughts?

Clear Sky

Thomas doubted.
Peter denied.
Haley whined.
What's your story?

When Thomas doubted, Jesus came to him to show him the wounds in his hands. He gave Thomas visible proof, but He also said those who would believe without seeing would have greater blessing. (John 20:29)

When Peter denied, Jesus went to him to forgive him. He encouraged Peter so that shame would not keep him from becoming the Rock that God had created him to be. (John 21)

When I whined about my life, Jesus came to me and gave me a new one. That is part of what He said He would do, that He would give us life to the full. That means He will fill us up with the life He created for us, which could look very different than the life we try to plan. In following Him, He has given me things I never asked for, so that in the drama of this story He could be revealed.

Once upon a time I said yes to the Lord and decided to follow Him with all of my heart, mind, and soul. He began to fulfill His purposes and plans in me. He healed me and set me free. He equipped me and gave me tools to do His work. He made known to me His plans so that I could walk in them. For every enemy that came against me, He gave me help and hope. He allowed the pain that would heal me and the grace that would empower me. He was true to His Word and faithful to accomplish all He has promised.

As He gave me purpose, He gave me blessings. He gave me the mist of Victoria Falls on my face. He let me see a herd of baboons marching across the Serengeti of Africa. Out of my airplane window I viewed with my own eye the tip of Mount Everest. I've tasted empanadas in Bolivia, Pad Thai on the bank of the River Kwai in Thailand, and the best tea on the planet in Sri Lanka. I've been in the Garden of Gethsemane, the Colosseum in Rome, and to each of the Seven Churches of Revelation in Turkey. I saw the valley where Jacob wrestled with God in Jordan, the cave where the Dead Sea Scrolls were found, and the Great Pyramids of Egypt.

I've seen the tombs of Peter and John (and Christopher Columbus), and the empty grave of Jesus of Nazareth who is the Savior of the world. God has given me a sunset in Bali, chocolate in Vienna, a train ride across the German landscape, the ocean view from the Cliffs of Mohr in Ireland, the nighttime skyline in Hong Kong, fireworks across the Sky in India, castles in Eastern Europe, and steps taken nearly within throwing distance of the shadow of Mt. Ararat. I've heard prayers and praises to God in languages of many tongues, and I have loved them all and cried through many. He has proven His presence time and time and time again, and I will live my days proclaiming Him.

With the Great Sphinx of Giza.

My sunset in Bali.

At the amphitheater in Ephesus mentioned in Acts 19.

Is there anything in your life that keeps you from fully believing, fully following, or fully trusting Jesus? The Scripture says that He is the same today, yesterday, and forever. (Hebrews 13:8) You and I are not apostles as Thomas and Peter were, but Jesus is the same for us as He was for them. He will intervene in our lives when ...

we humble ourselves,
unclench our fists,
let go of our grasp,
and let Him lift us to the heart change,
the attitude change, and the life change
He wants to do in us.

You will not prove Him or disprove Him through arguments or logic, as long as arguments and logic rely on human understanding. God is more than we can fully grasp. You must experience Him for your faith to grow.

In putting my hope in God's goodness, not just in God's answer, and in taking very tangible, practical, and sometimes painful steps to "let go and let God," I have developed a taste for the Sky. My hunger for the Land has changed, and my life has been transformed. I can see the beauty in God's plans, His goodness in His ways, and His consistency in His Word.

All I had to give was the tiniest, foot dragging, "yes." And, He gave me both Land and Sky.

Believe and see ...

"I waited patiently for the Lord;
He inclined to me and heard my cry.
He drew me up from the pit of destruction,
out of the miry bog,
and set my feet upon a rock,
making my steps secure.
He put a new song in my mouth,
a song of praise to our God.
Many will see and fear,
and put their trust in the Lord.
Blessed is the man who makes
the Lord his trust,
who does not turn to the proud,
to those who go astray after a lie!
You have multiplied, O Lord my God,
your wondrous deeds and your thoughts toward us;
none can compare with you!
I will proclaim and tell of them,
yet they are more than can be told.
In sacrifice and offering you have not delighted,
but you have given me an open ear.
Burnt offering and sin offering
you have not required.
Then I said, 'Behold, I have come;
in the scroll of the book it is written of me:
I delight to do your will, O my God;
your law is within my heart.'
I have told the glad news of deliverance
in the great congregation;
behold, I have not restrained my lips,
as you know, O Lord.
I have not hidden your deliverance within my heart;
I have spoken of your faithfulness and your salvation;
I have not concealed your steadfast love and your faithfulness
from the great congregation."
(Psalm 40:1-10, ESV)

What's Your Story?

Do you believe? If you struggle with belief ... are you asking your questions or just making assumptions?

Is there something God has been showing you? Is He prompting you to say "yes" to something? What's stopping you?

Haley L. Scully

ACKNOWLEDGMENTS

Every time frame and people group in our lives shapes us. We become more of who we are because of who walks beside us. These family and friends have been part of the story I share in this book, and I am thankful.

The Family –

Some of them are already in heaven and I don't think they are going to be able to read this, but I could never have a page titled "Acknowledgements" in regards to my life without their names being listed. My grandparents, John and Authula "Toots" Scully – anyone who has been around me for any amount of time will have heard me talk about my Granny Toots. She still walks beside me every day of my life. My Grandpa, Corky Harmon, and Aunt Karla Dilbeck – I don't get to see these four with my eyes, but I still see them constantly with my heart. Thanks to my Grandma Bonnie who always praises Jesus over every big and small good in our lives. I got to see her hold this book in her hands. My life is an extension of God's faithfulness to her. Mom and Dad are the lead characters in the story God has given me, and without their encouragement to trust Him and do the hard things, I would probably be in a puddle somewhere. To Chris, Leigh, Jordan, Kaitlyn, and Shawn for being my people in good times and bad. Thanks to my Harmon's who taught me how to love "a bushel and a peck" and to my Scully's who taught me that sarcasm and sass are virtues.

The Magnolias –

Thanks for being women of God to follow. Thanks for always praying for all of us kids, rejoicing in each of our victories, and crying for us when we hurt. We have been so blessed by your strength, your devotion, and your protection of each other. Your love for one another encourages me to love my friends better. Your prayers have made me stronger.

The Lady Birds –

Who knew after we went and looked at that first house that we would stay friends forever? I'm so thankful we were all so broke that we couldn't overcome objections to being grown women trying to live in the same house together. Your patience and love changed my story. Thank you, Kim Brown, Sarah Casas-Cutrell and MariAnne Falls-Williamson for sharpening, inspiring, and praying with me.

The Seminarians –

I am incredibly grateful for the encouragement and guidance from mentors, professors and friends at Southwestern Baptist Theological Seminary. Your heart to serve the Lord and pour into the lives of others changed me. I count those days with all of you as one of my greatest blessings. I still geek out when I see each of you. Everywhere I go in ministry, your teaching, mentoring, and friendship from that time goes with me.

The teachers: Dr. Ian Jones, Dr. Scott Floyd, Dr. Mike McGuire, Dr. Elias Moitinho, Dr. Dana Wicker, Dr. Richard Ross, Dr. Wesley Black, Dr. Johnny Derouen.

And the friends who taught me so much … The long talks over coffee and M&M's, leading Youth Lab, trying to study, learning that Paul supposedly said cuss words, laughing, crying, and seeking God's will in our lives, heartbreaks, and futures … it makes me nearly sick with joy to think back on that time with you guys: Ryan and Jessica Walling – Thanks for letting me be part of a few moments of your incredible story. Your steps of faith helped me take mine. Justin Arnold, Krissie Lain Garland, Kym Tucker McKenzie, Jana Stanfield Fowler, Kayla Hawthorne Eaton. Thanks for being my friends, even though I only had the one jean skirt.

The Ministry Mentors –

Thank you for opening doors and leading me – sometimes dragging me – through them. You have encouraged me and taught me so much more than you even meant to teach me, and many times when you didn't even know I was paying attention. I am incredibly grateful for your testimonies and leadership. Honestly, no words would ever be enough here. Phillip Prather, Norma Brown, Rick and Kathy Ragan, Dr. Steve Hunter, June Hunt, Susan Jackson, Ray Alary, Colleen Shoemaker.

The International Friends –

I came to your countries, your cities, your churches, and, many times, your homes. You cared for me, you protected me, you encouraged me. Your kindness and love has grown my faith in our Lord. Your stories are an inspiration and your friendship a gift.

The Fox Force –

Thank you Dana, Dotti, and Jenny who walked beside me in that first cave and sat by me out in the sunshine. I wouldn't trade any of it, well maybe some of it, but not the parts with you three.

The Editors –

Thank you Mom and Dad and Tiffany Blake for reading this ahead and helping me fix errors or confusion that I could no longer see on these pages. And, thank you Lindsey Morris for taking the first professional editing crack at this. You helped me believe this could be a real thing. Colleen Shoemaker, (and Tess and Kevin) thanks for doing the wrap up! If people can read through it without getting honked up on grammar errors, it's because of you. Your help, friendship, and long-distance laughs are such a gift to me! If history is any indicator, the next time I see you it will be someplace neither one of us ever wanted to go … but, He will be there waiting for us.

Haley L. Scully

"Once Upon a Time" Scripture References, pages 129-130

"Once upon a time there was a little girl who never dreamed of going anywhere. She liked where she was. She didn't like everything about where she was, but she certainly didn't want to be anywhere else. She had grown up believing in the King who had come to save her (**John 3:16**), and she tried her best to honor Him, as little she knew of Him.

But then one day, as she was right in the middle of denying Him, He called to her by name and spoke tenderly to her. He knew her. She began to see Him with her own eyes, and see Him for who he really was (**Mark 14:66-72, Hosea 2:14-17**). She had believed He was the King. She had been obedient to Him because of

John 3:16 — "For God so loved the world, that he gave his only Son, that whoever believes in him should not perish but have eternal life."

Mark 14:69-70 — "And the servant girl saw him and began again to say to the bystanders, 'this man is one of them.' But again he denied it. And after a little while the bystanders again said to Peter, 'Certainly you are one of them, for you are a Galilean.'"

Hosea 2:14-17 — "Therefore, behold, I will allure her, and bring her into the wilderness, and speak tenderly to her. And there I will give her vineyards and make the valley of Achor a door of hope. And there she shall answer as in the days of her youth, as at the time when she came out of the land of Egypt. And in that day, declares the LORD, you will call me 'My Husband,' and no longer will you call me 'My Baal.' For I will remove the names of the Baals from her mouth, and they shall be remembered by name no more."

that, but now she began to fall in love with Him. So, when He asked her to come away with Him, she went (**Mark 6:31**). While there, He showed her that He was actually the King of Everywhere, not just of where she was born (**1 Corinthians 10:26**).

She thought she had known that all along, but she realized she wasn't really going the way she should go, if that is what she truly believed (**Proverbs 22:6**). He showed her that there was nowhere she could ever go where He wasn't there, waiting on her (**Deuteronomy 31:6**). He told her that He had loved her and had taken care of her all along, because He had plans for her (**Jeremiah 29:11**). He became her shelter and protector (**Psalm 18:2**).

Mark 6:31 – "And he said to them, 'Come away by yourselves to a desolate place and rest a while.' For many were coming and going, and they had no leisure even to eat."

1 Corinthians 10:26 – "For 'the earth is the Lord's, and the fullness thereof.'"

Proverbs 22:6 – "Train up a child in the way he should go; even when he is old he will not depart from it."

Deuteronomy 31:6 – "Be strong and courageous. Do not fear or be in dread of them, for it is the LORD your God who goes with you. He will not leave you or forsake you."

Jeremiah 29:11 – "For I know the plans I have for you, declares the LORD, plans for welfare and not for evil, to give you a future and a hope."

Psalm 18:2 – "The LORD is my rock and my fortress and my deliverer, my God, my rock, in whom I take refuge, my shield, and the horn of my salvation, my stronghold."

Sometimes He led her through a wilderness to humble and test her and provided her manna when there was nothing else (**Deuteronomy 8:16**). He would send her rain when she prayed for it (**James 5:18**). He would make His face to shine upon her (**Numbers 6:24-26**). He counted her tears and comforted her when news of loved ones from home made her cry (**Psalm 56:8**).

He strengthened her, dealt bountifully with her, and gave her rest (**Isaiah 41:10, Psalm 116:7**). When she lifted her eyes to the hills, she could always see Him there (**Psalm 121:1-2**). In the morning, he reminded her that He loved her and told her the way she should go because she trusted Him (**Psalm 143:8**). Where He went, she went. His people

Deuteronomy 8:16 – "(He) who fed you in the wilderness with manna that your fathers did not know, that he might humble you and test you, to do you good in the end."

James 5:18 – "Then he prayed again, and heaven gave rain, and the earth bore its fruit."

Numbers 6:24-26 – "The LORD bless you and keep you; the LORD make His face shine upon you and be gracious to you; the Lord lift up His countenance upon you and give you peace."

Psalm 56:8 – "You have kept count of my tossings; put my tears in your bottle. Are they not in your book?"

Isaiah 41:10 – "… fear not, for I am with you; be not dismayed, for I am your God; I will strengthen you, I will help you, I will uphold you with my righteous right hand."

Psalm 116:7 – "Return, O my soul, to your rest; for the LORD has dealt bountifully with you."

Psalm 121:1-2 – "I lift up my eyes to the hills. From where does my help come? My help comes from the LORD, who made heaven and earth."

Psalm 143:8 – "Let me hear in the morning of your steadfast love, for in you I trust. Make me know the way I should go, for to you I lift up my soul."

were her people (**Ruth 1:16**). If she had been longing to return to the Land from which she had come, she could have gone. She stayed with Him in the new Land, and He was proud of her (**Hebrews 11:15-16**).

When she told Him her foot was slipping, He supported her, and when her anxiety was great, He consoled her and gave her joy (**Psalm 94:18-19**). When she put her hope in Him, He taught her the paths she should take, and her heart was not sick (**Psalm 25:4-5, Proverbs 13:12**). When there were giants, He gave her stones to sling (**1 Samuel 17:40**). When there were words to be said, He placed them on her tongue (**Jeremiah 1:9**). When there were journeys to take, He lit her path by day and by

Ruth 1:16 – "But Ruth said, 'Do not urge me to leave you or to return from following you. For where you go I will go, and where you lodge I will lodge. Your people shall be my people, and your God my God.'"

Hebrews 11:15-16 – "If they had been thinking of that land from which they had gone out, they would have had opportunity to return. But as it is, they desire a better country, that is, a heavenly one. Therefore God is not ashamed to be called their God, for he has prepared for them a city."

Psalm 94:18-19 – "When I thought, 'My foot slips,' your steadfast love, O LORD, held me up. When the cares of my heart are many, your consolations cheer my soul."

Psalm 25:4-5 – "Make me to know your ways, O LORD; teach me your paths. Lead me in your truth and teach me, for you are the God of my salvation; for you I wait all the day long."

Proverbs 13:12 –"Hope deferred makes the heart sick, but a desire fulfilled is a tree of life."

1 Samuel 17:40 –"Then he took his staff in his hand, chose five smooth stones from the brook and put them in his shepherd's pouch. His sling was in his hand, he approached the Philistine."

Jeremiah 1:9 – "Then the LORD put out his hand and touched my mouth. And the Lord said to me, 'Behold, I have put my words in your mouth.'"

night (**Exodus 13:21**). He did all of this because she was weak, but He was strong (**2 Samuel 22:33**). He saved her, quieted her, and sang over her (**Zephaniah 3:17**). He gave her a new heart and courage (**Ezekiel 36:26, Joshua 1:7**). Then He led her on a new path, lighting the way as He smoothed the road ahead of her (**Isaiah 42:16**). That is what God does."

God is unchanging. These specific books in the Bible were written to people other than me, but they demonstrate who God is, was, and will be.

We can know God's character and consistency through His Word, and we can apply it to our lives today and always.

All Bible verses from the ESV.

Exodus 13:21 – "And the LORD went before them by day in a pillar of cloud to lead them along the way, and by night in a pillar of fire to give them light, that they might travel by day and by night."

2 Samuel 22:33 – "This God is my strong refuge and has made my way blameless."

Zephaniah 3:17 – "The LORD your God is in your midst, a Mighty One who will save. He will rejoice over you with gladness; he will quiet you by his love; he will exult over you with loud singing."

Ezekiel 36:26 – "I will give you a new heart, and a new spirit I will put within you. And I will remove the heart of stone from your flesh and give you a heart of flesh."

Joshua 1:7 – "Only be strong and very courageous, being careful to do according to all the law that Moses my servant commanded you. Do not turn from it to the right hand or to the left, that you may have good success wherever you go."

Isaiah 42:16 – "And I will lead the blind in a way that they do not know, in paths that they have not known I will guide them. I will turn the darkness before them into light, the rough places into level ground. These are the things I do, and I do not forsake them."

Haley L. Scully

Made in the USA
Columbia, SC
30 August 2018